Criminal Litigation,

Evidence and Sentencing

CW01430523

Criminal Litigation,

Evidence and Sentencing

Rory Clarke

Rosalind Earis

Lulu.

Copyright © Rory Clarke and Rosalind Earis 2014

The right of Rory Clarke and Rosalind Earis to be identified as the authors of this work has been asserted by them in accordance with the Copyright, Designs and Patents Act 1988.

First published in Great Britain in 2014

This edition published in Great Britain in 2014

All rights reserved. No part of this publication may be reproduced, stored in a retrieval system, or transmitted, in any form or by any means without the prior permission in writing of the authors, or as expressly permitted by law, or under terms agreed with the appropriate reprographics organisation.

ISBN 978-1-291-22731-4

Foreword

For the last thirteen years, there have been two recurring questions from my BVC and BPTC students facing the Himalayan feat of learning Criminal Litigation, Evidence and Sentencing: *"is there a good textbook available?"* and *"how am I supposed to revise all of that?"*. These requests have become even more pertinent since 2012 when the Bar Standards Board made criminal litigation one of the new centrally set assessments. Teaching to an in-house exam is no longer possible (and good riddance I say) but the introduction of this level playing field has made the students' plea for a decent textbook all the more apposite. At last, I have the answer to their prayers (and mine) and it was worth waiting for; Rory Clarke and Rosalind Earis have produced a vital tome for every BPTC student and frankly anyone in practice who wants an accessible, reliable guide.

This text book is designed as a one-stop-shop for any student aspiring to ascend to the summit in this centrally set subject. From the outset, this book will provide an invaluable overview and, when detailed knowledge is more relevant, it will become increasingly useful as a consolidation tool and the ultimate revision guide. Any candid BPTC student will tell you that scant knowledge of the subject will not suffice. Detail is required to tackle the short answer questions and the clever way in which this text book has been designed will aid that process of learning immeasurably. Personally, my favourite part is the mnemonic for the s.101 (1) gateways at 15.3 and Section 5 on Sentencing is *"Outstanding"*.

Rory Clarke and **Rosalind Earis** are two of the most industrious, magnanimous individuals I have met in many years of teaching aspiring barristers. This book is testament to their combined talents and their attention to detail. Not only will I be recommending it to all my students but there is one at the bottom of my court bag.

Lynda Gibbs
Barrister, BPTC Course Leader
Kaplan Law School

Introduction

During our BPTC we realised that what a BPTC student really needs is a concise, no-frills overview to the entire criminal course. We were taught a lot about criminal procedure, using a number of practitioner texts and conventional textbooks, but we found nothing available which contained all of the material all in one place, and in a format short enough to use for revision. That is why we wrote this book.

Whether you are seeking an initial overview of a particular topic or worrying about how you will ever learn the entire BPTC Criminal Litigation and Evidence syllabus in time for the exam, this is the book for you. It has been designed to be:

- An overview to criminal procedure, as taught on the BPTC;
- The perfect revision guide to help you pass the 2013-2014 BPTC Criminal Litigation and Evidence exam;
- A useful aide memoire for fledgling criminal lawyers, covering the basics without going into the detail of the practitioner texts.

However, this book is not intended to be a practitioner text or conventional textbook. It will not teach you criminal procedure from scratch, and it does not go into the depth of a practitioner text. Its role is to help you understand and then learn (where necessary memorise) those aspects of criminal litigation and the rules of evidence that are required to pass the BPTC exam.

This book has its origins in our revision notes, which served us well in the Criminal Litigation and Evidence exam. However, this book could not have been produced from our notes alone. It is the product of many hours of work – checking and updating the law, as well as improving the format – and we would like to thank all those who helped us, and especially Lynda Gibbs and Jacqui Beeley of Kaplan Law School. Their constant support and constructive criticism have been invaluable.

We wish you luck in your studies and hope that this book assists in bringing you success on the BPTC.

Rory Clarke

Rosalind Earis

Using This Book

Content

This book is structured to mirror the BPTC syllabus, and the chapters are organised accordingly. Sections that appear in italic print marked *"outline only"* are those which the syllabus does not require you to know in depth.

Anything that you need to know for the exam, including specific sections of an Act and case names, is in the main body of the text. The statutory provisions from which the procedure is derived have been included as footnotes to assist anyone who wishes to delve further; however, for the purposes of the exam it is not necessary to know anything that appears in a footnote. Additionally, procedural rules and legal exceptions which are not relevant to the task in hand have been omitted from this text. Statutory provisions are often paraphrased for clarity and simplicity, and case law is not cited unless necessary for the exam.

Layout

The layout has been designed to assist in memorising the contents of the text and so:

- Important words appear in **bold**;
- Paragraphs are not justified (the edges are not straight) and are laid out to assist those who memorise by visualisation;
- Numbers and abbreviations are used wherever possible rather than text;
- All people are referred to as *"he"* throughout for brevity.

Abbreviations

Common abbreviations:

D	Defendant / the defence / the accused / the offender
Co-D	Co-defendant
P	Prosecutor / the prosecution
Youth-D	Juvenile defendant
Non-D	Non-defendant

Other Abbreviations:

BA 1976	Bail Act 1976
CAA 1968	Criminal Appeals Act 1968
CDA 1998	Crime and Disorder Act 1998
CFO	Commit Further Offences
CJA	Criminal Justice Act
CJPOA 1994	Criminal Justice and Public Order Act 1994
CPA 1865	Criminal Procedure Act 1865
CPIA 1996	Criminal Procedure and Investigations Act 1996
CrimPR	Criminal Procedure Rules
CTL	Custody Time Limit
CYPA 1933	Children and Young Persons Act 1933
DTO	Detention and Training Order
ECHR	European Convention on Human Rights
FTS	Fail to Surrender
IPP	Imprisonment for Public Protection
IWW	Interfere with Witnesses
LPP	Legal Professional Privilege
MCA 1980	Magistrates' Courts Act 1980
PACE 1984	Police and Criminal Evidence Act 1984
PCC(S)A 2000	Power of Criminal Courts (Sentencing) Act 2000
PII	Public Interest Immunity
POA 1985	Prosecution of Offences Act 1985
PSR	Pre-sentence Report
SOA 2003	Sexual Offences Act 2003
SSO	Suspended Sentence Order
V	Victim
YJCEA 1999	Youth Justice and Criminal Evidence Act 1999
YOT	Youth Offending Team
YRO	Youth Rehabilitation Order

Contents

Section 5 – Sentencing

Section 6 – Appeals

Section 1

Overview

1. Overview of Criminal Procedure

1.1 The classification of offences (indictable, either-way and summary)

Summary offences can **only be tried in the Magistrates' Court**: if charged with a summary offence D has no right to a jury trial. Summary offences are less serious crimes punishable by non-custodial sentences or short custodial sentences.

Indictable only offences **can only be tried in the Crown Court**, by a jury. Indictable only offences are serious offences demanding more serious sentences.

Offences triable either way can be tried **either** in the Magistrates' Court **or** by jury in the Crown Court (see 4.5 for details of the allocation procedure). Either-way offences are those which could be less or more serious depending on their facts.

1.2 The court structure in England and Wales

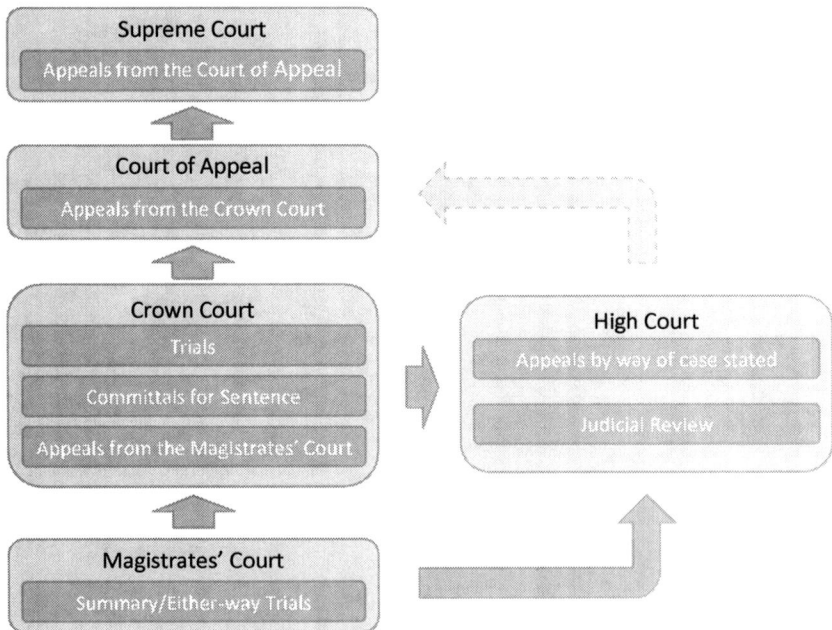

Supreme Court
Appeals from the Court of Appeal

Court of Appeal
Appeals from the Crown Court

Crown Court
Trials
Committals for Sentence
Appeals from the Magistrates' Court

High Court
Appeals by way of case stated
Judicial Review

Magistrates' Court
Summary/Either-way Trials

1.3 How a criminal case progresses

The diagram below outlines how a criminal case will progress if **D is an adult:**

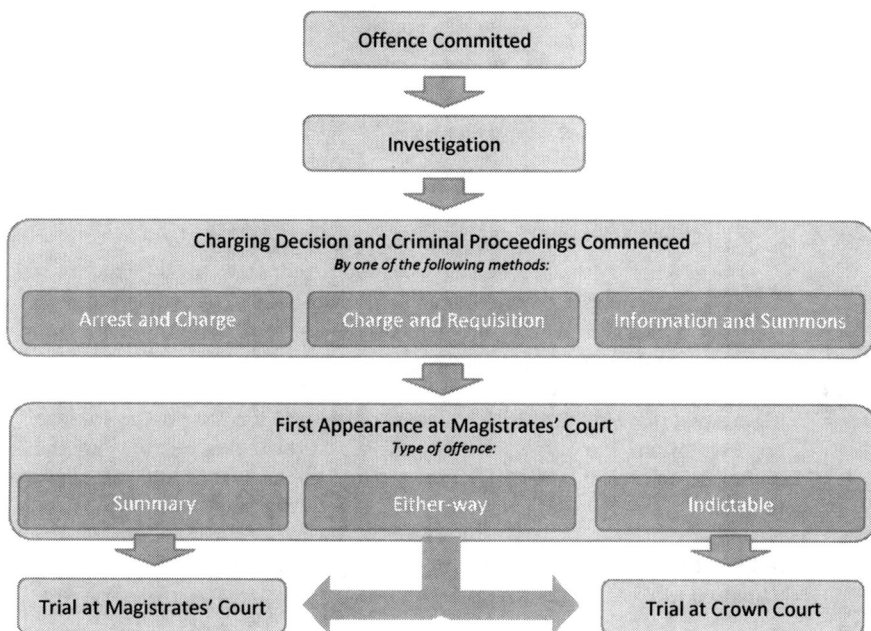

```
┌─────────────────────────┐
│    Offence Committed     │
└─────────────────────────┘
            ↓
┌─────────────────────────┐
│      Investigation       │
└─────────────────────────┘
            ↓
┌───────────────────────────────────────────────────────┐
│  Charging Decision and Criminal Proceedings Commenced  │
│            By one of the following methods:            │
│  ┌──────────────┐ ┌──────────────┐ ┌────────────────┐ │
│  │Arrest and    │ │Charge and    │ │Information and │ │
│  │Charge        │ │Requisition   │ │Summons         │ │
│  └──────────────┘ └──────────────┘ └────────────────┘ │
└───────────────────────────────────────────────────────┘
            ↓
┌───────────────────────────────────────────────────────┐
│          First Appearance at Magistrates' Court        │
│                    Type of offence:                    │
│  ┌──────────────┐ ┌──────────────┐ ┌────────────────┐ │
│  │   Summary    │ │  Either-way  │ │   Indictable   │ │
│  └──────────────┘ └──────────────┘ └────────────────┘ │
└───────────────────────────────────────────────────────┘
     ↓                    ↔                      ↓
┌──────────────────────┐            ┌──────────────────────┐
│Trial at Magistrates' │            │  Trial at Crown Court │
│       Court          │            │                      │
└──────────────────────┘            └──────────────────────┘
```

The process is similar for a Youth-D, although in general **all types of offence will be tried in the Youth Court** when D is a youth. A Youth-D can be tried in the Crown Court in certain circumstances (see 21.4 below).

1.4 Funding criminal cases (the general structure of funding arrangements)

Prosecution

Prosecutions are funded by whoever brings them. For most cases, this is the (publicly funded) Crown Prosecution Service or another publicly-funded body (e.g. HMRC). Where a private individual brings a prosecution, he bears the cost but may be refunded from central funds regardless of success.

If convicted, D may be ordered to pay all or part of the P costs, dependent on D's means.

Defence

Defence funding is provided by the Criminal Defence Service. D will receive free legal assistance and representation, subject to passing the **interests of justice test**, and a **means test** (the latter only for Magistrates' Court cases):

- **Interests of justice test** (for all cases) = **does D's case deserve legal aid?** Consider e.g.:
    - Whether D would face a custodial sentence, lose his livelihood or his reputation;
    - Whether there will be a substantial question of law in the proceedings;
    - Whether D will understand the proceedings;
    - Whether the proceedings will require witnesses to be traced or interviewed, or whether an expert will need to be cross-examined;
    - Whether it is in the interests of someone else that D be represented.[1]

- **Means test** (for Magistrates' Court cases only) = is D too poor to pay for legal representation? Some Ds will automatically pass the means test (e.g. youths and those on certain benefits). Those earning over around £21,000 are unlikely to pass.

    If D fails this test and pays all or part of his legal costs, he may be refunded if acquitted.

1.5 The importance and application of the Criminal Procedure Rules; the overriding objective and the case management functions of the court

The Criminal Procedure Rules (CrimPR) are a concise consolidation into one document of all previous procedure rules, practice directions and guidance codes.

Part 1 of the CrimPR states the **overriding objective**: that **criminal cases be dealt with justly**, which includes:
- Acquitting the innocent and convicting the guilty;
- Dealing with the P and the D fairly;
- Recognising the rights of D, particularly those under Art 6 ECHR;
- Respecting the interests of witnesses, victims and jurors and keeping them informed of the progress of the case;
- Dealing with the case efficiently and expeditiously;
- Ensuring that appropriate information is available to the court when bail and sentence are considered;

---

[1] Found here: http://www.justice.gov.uk/legal-aid/assess-your-clients-eligibility/interests-of-justice-test.

- Dealing with the case in ways that take into account:
  - The gravity of the offence alleged;
  - The complexity of what is in issue;
  - The severity of the consequences for D and others affected;
  - The needs of other cases.

Part 3 of the CrimPR sets out the court's case management functions, and states that **the court must further the overriding objective by actively managing the case.**

The court's case management powers are wide: it may give any direction and take any step actively to manage a case, as long as it is not inconsistent with legislation. The aim is to ensure that the case progresses speedily, but fairly.

Section 2

Criminal investigations, commencement of proceedings and pre-trial issues

2. Preliminaries to Prosecution

All police investigations must be carried out in accordance with the PACE codes of conduct:

A: Powers of stop and search
B: Searching premises
C: Detention, treatment and questioning
D: Identification of people
E: Tape recording of interviews
F: Visual recording of interviews with sound
G: Powers of arrest
H: Terrorism

Failure to adhere to these codes **may** result in evidence being excluded as inadmissible, or even in the entire P case being stayed as an abuse of process.

2.2 The provisions of Code C.10 (cautions and special warnings) and Code C.11 (interviews)

Code C.10: cautions

"You do not have to say anything, but it may harm your defence if you do not mention when questioned something which you later rely on in court.
Anything you do say may be given in evidence"

It does not matter if the words used are slightly different from the standard caution, as long as the meaning is the same.

A caution **must** be given to:

"A person whom there are grounds to suspect of an offence"
BEFORE
"Any questions about an offence, or further questions if the answers provide the grounds for suspicion" are put to them,
IF
"Either the suspect's answers or silence may be given in evidence to a court in a prosecution".

A caution is not necessary when questions are general (e.g. asking someone who he is,.

"Grounds for suspicion" means **reasonable and objective grounds** to suspect the person of a criminal offence.

A caution must also be given on arrest, unless:
- It is **impracticable** to do so because of the arrestee's condition or behaviour at the time; or
- The arrestee has **already been cautioned** immediately before being arrested.

The caution should be re-administered after any significant break in questioning. If originally administered to a child or vulnerable adult when no other adult was present, it should be repeated in the presence of an appropriate adult.

If the person being questioned is not under arrest, they must be informed that they are free to leave at any time.

If the person being questioned has requested a solicitor but that request has been denied, then a shorter caution should be used and **no inferences will be drawn from silence** (see below). The shorter caution is:

> *"You do not have to say anything, but anything you do say may be given in evidence"*

Code C.10: special warnings

If D fails to answer **certain key questions** when asked by the police, the court may infer that D is guilty of the offence of which he is suspected. This is an **adverse inference**[2] (see chapter 17). Before the court will be allowed to draw an adverse inference, the police must D give a **special warning**.

In giving a special warning, the police must tell D:
- What offence is being investigated;
- What fact D is being asked to account for;
- That this fact may be due to him taking part in the commission of the offence;
- That a court may draw a proper inference if D fails or refuses to account for this fact;
- That a record is being made of the interview and it may be given in evidence if D is brought to trial.

---

[2] ss.36-37 CJPOA 1994 - the court may draw *"such inferences as appear proper"*.

A special warning will be given in relation to certain key questions, when:
- The restriction on adverse inferences does not apply; **and**
- The suspect was arrested by a constable; **and either**:
  - He refuses to account for **an object, marks or substances** on his person, clothes, possessions or in the place of arrest; **or**
  - He refuses to account for his **presence at a crime scene**.

Code C.11: interviews

An interview is **any questioning of a person regarding his involvement or suspected involvement in a criminal offence**. It **must** take place under caution.

The interviewer **must** inform D of the nature of the offence alleged. An interview should always be in a police station **unless** delay would lead to any of:
- Interference with evidence;
- Harm to a person;
- The alerting of suspects;
- The hindering of recovery of property.

D has a right to:
- See a solicitor (although not necessarily present in interview). This right **can be delayed for a maximum of 36 hours**. A delay of up to 36 hours must be authorised by a superintendent. This right can only be delayed for these reasons:
  - To prevent interference with evidence, harm to a person, the alerting of suspects, or the hindering of recovery of property (i.e. same as above); or
  - The solicitor has agreed to advise, but waiting for his arrival would cause unreasonable delay to the investigation; or
  - D has refused the duty solicitor.
- Have someone informed of his arrest. This can be delayed on same grounds as legal advice above; and
- Consult the PACE codes.

An accurate record must be made of each interview. Normally this will be done by tape-recording the interview, but it can be done by writing down a verbatim or otherwise accurate account of the interview. The record should include the time and place of interview, any breaks taken, and the names of those present.

If D says something significant not on the tape, the interviewer will caution D and then state what D said and ask D to comment. The interviewer should make a written record and ask D to sign it.

An interview should stop when enough evidence has been gathered and all appropriate questions asked.

No answer may be elicited by oppression. The interviewer should not tell D what will happen if he does or does not answer, unless directly asked.

2.3 The provisions of Code D.3 (identification by witnesses)

Code D of PACE lays down the regime for ensuring that ID procedures are fair. Paragraph D.3 deals with visual ID.

A record should be made of a witness's description of D before he takes part in any ID procedure.

There are 3 main categories of ID procedure:

1. When the ID of the **suspect is known to the police** and he is **available** then any of the following may be used:
   - **Video ID**: the witness is shown images of a suspect, together with ID of **at least 8 other people** who resemble the suspect. Images can be moving or still.
   - **ID parade**: the suspect is put into a line-up of **at least 8 people**. The witness views the line-up.
   - **Group ID**: the suspect is put into an **informal group of people**, e.g. walking through a shopping centre or in a queue at a bus station. The witness is present at the scene.
   - **Confrontation**: the suspect is shown to the witness. In certain circumstances a screen may be used to prevent the suspect seeing the witness. Normally the suspect's solicitor, friend or interpreter must be present during the confrontation.

2. Where the ID of the suspect is **known to the police** but he is **not available**, the ID officer may arrange a **video ID** (see above). Failure or refusal to participate may be treated as not being available.

3. When the ID of the suspect is **not known to the police** the witness may be:
   - Taken to a particular neighbourhood (*"street ID"*) and asked if he can see the suspect; **or**
   - Given an opportunity to look through existing police photographs.

Known   =   Sufficient information is known to the police to justify arrest of a particular person for suspected involvement in the offence.

Available   =   The suspect is:
   - Immediately available or will be in a reasonably short time; **and**
   - Is willing to take an effective part in the ID procedure.

Dock identification, where a witness identifies D in the dock at court, should not generally be allowed as it is considered leading. Dock ID may be permissible when D refuses to attend ID parade or renders the parade impracticable (e.g. by changing his appearance).

2.4 The different powers of search and arrest

Search

Police can search persons and vehicles for: **stolen goods**, **articles** for use in offences, and **weapons**. But they must:

- Have reasonable grounds for carrying out the search; **and**
- Be in uniform or provide ID; **and**
- Carry out the search at or near the place where person/vehicle is stopped; **and**
- Not remove a suspect's clothes in public, other than outer clothes.

Arrest without warrant

A **constable** can arrest without a warrant:[3]

- Anyone committing or about to commit a definite offence;
- Anyone he has reasonable grounds to suspect is committing or is about to commit a definite offence;
- Anyone he has reasonable grounds to suspect has already committed a definite offence;
- Anyone he has reasonable grounds to suspect has committed a suspected offence.

AND, it must be necessary to arrest the person for any of these reasons:

- To obtain the name or address of the suspect;
- To stop the suspect doing something else unlawful;
- To protect someone;
- To allow investigation of the case;
- To prevent the suspect getting away.

A civilian can arrest someone in much more limited circumstances, i.e. **only if**:

- That person **has committed** an offence or is in **the act of committing an offence**; **and**
- The offence is **indictable-only**; **and**
- A constable cannot do it instead, **and**
- Arrest is necessary to prevent the person in question:

---

[3] s.24 PACE 1984.

- Causing physical injury; **or**
- Suffering physical injury; **or**
- Causing loss of or damage to property; **or**
- Getting away.

Arrest with warrant

A warrant is **normally issued by Magistrates** after hearing an application from a police officer. The suspect must be over 18.

A warrant can also be issued by the court (= **bench warrant**) where D does not attend for trial or answer bail. A bench warrant can be **backed for bail** (= D will be arrested but released on bail) or **not backed for bail** (D will then be kept in custody until he is brought before a court).

For an arrest (with or without warrant) to be effected properly, the suspect must be:
- Informed by a police officer that he is under arrest, and **what for**, as soon as practicable.[4] (Note: if the reason given is illegal, it is irrelevant that a good reason did exist); **or**
- Physically seized (suspect must be informed as soon as practicable **what for**); **or**
- Given a combination of words and conduct which make it clear that force will be used to prevent him leaving.

An arrestee can be searched.

An arrestee must **either**:
- Be taken to a **police station** as soon as practicable, unless it is reasonable to carry out other investigations first (e.g. search premises); **or**
- Be released on **street bail** (= released immediately but given a time to report to a police station).

If detention will exceed 6 hours, the suspect should be taken to a designated station. It is legal to arrest a suspect on a **holding charge** (= charge for a minor offence made so that the police can interrogate him for other more serious matters), as long as he was liable to legal arrest at the time.

2.5 The role of the Crown Prosecution Service

The Crown Prosecution Service (CPS) is a government department responsible for prosecuting those charged with a criminal offence. It is not the only public prosecuting

---

[4] s.28 PACE 1984.

body, but it brings the vast majority of prosecutions in England and Wales. Its head is the Director of Public Prosecutions (DPP).

The CPS is completely independent of the police: the police investigate and gather evidence, which is then passed to the CPS to use in a prosecution.

The CPS:
- Advises the police on cases for possible prosecution;
- Reviews cases submitted by the police;
- Determines what charge to bring in **all indictable offences, most either-way offences** and **some summary offences** (the police do the rest);
- Prepares cases for court;
- Presents cases at court.

The CPS employs some in-house advocates, but much of its advocacy work (especially in the Crown Court) is briefed out to self-employed barristers working from Chambers.

2.6 The different forms of commencing criminal proceedings

Arrest and charge = D is arrested for an offence. He is usually interviewed, and other investigations will be carried out. If the evidence against him is sufficient, he is charged with (= formally accused of) an offence at the police station and either kept in custody to appear before a court, or bailed to appear before a court on a specified date, to answer the charge.

Written charge and requisition[5] = D receives a written notice that he is being charged with an offence (the **written charge**), and a notice that he must appear before the Magistrates' Court to answer the charge (**the requisition**). This method replaced information and summons, although can only be used by **public prosecutors**. It can be used whether D was arrested or not.

Information and summons[6] = The old form of a written charge and requisition, now only available for **private prosecutors**. P will **lay an information** (= serve a document on the court or make an oral

---

[5] s.29 CJA 2003.
[6] s.1(1) MCA 1980.

presentation) setting out his accusation against D. The court, if satisfied by the information, will then issue either:

- A summons for D to appear before the Magistrates' court and answer the information; or
- A warrant for D's arrest.

A written charge and requisition is often used for driving matters or other minor matters where D was not caught at the scene. Arrest and charge is generally used for everything else.

3. Bail and Remands

3.1 The difference between adjournments and remands

Whenever a case is unfinished, the court makes a decision on what happens to the case and on what happens to D in the meantime.

Adjournment	=	Putting off the case until another time (e.g. *"adjourned until Monday morning"*). It refers to **what happens to the case**.
Remand	=	A decision on whether to release D on bail or remand in custody. It refers to **what happens to D**.

Usually the court will both adjourn the case and remand D. A **simple adjournment** is when the case is adjourned but D is neither remanded in custody nor on bail: he remains totally at liberty.

The Magistrates are free to choose between making a simple adjournment and remanding D when dealing with a summary offence, or when they are deferring sentence. However, a remand decision **must** be taken when:
- D was on bail or in custody when he first appeared in court; *or*
- D has been remanded at any time since.

The Crown Court **never** makes a simple adjournment.

3.2 Time limits applicable to defendants remanded in custody

To preserve the general right to liberty and ensure that cases are prepared quickly, D may only be remanded in custody for a certain amount of time before trial.

On remanding D in custody, the Magistrates' Court can commit him to detention at a police station for a maximum of **3 clear days** if it is necessary for inquiring into other offences. Once this need ceases D must be brought back before the court. D must be treated in accordance with the provisions of PACE 1984.

In general the maximum period that D can be remanded in prison by the Magistrates' Court is **8 clear days**. However, a longer period is permitted:
- For the period of any adjournment during the course of D's trial;
- Where D is unable to attend court owing to illness or an accident;
- Following conviction. D may be remanded in custody for up to **3 weeks**, in order to allow for inquiries to be made (e.g. for pre-sentence or medical reports) before deciding how to deal with him;

- Where the court decides to try an either-way offence summarily, but cannot do so immediately because it is not properly constituted, it may remand D in custody until a date when the court will be properly constituted;
- If D is already serving a custodial sentence, he may be remanded in custody for **28 clear days or until his release date, whichever is shorter.**

Additionally the Magistrates' Court may remand D for up to **28 clear days** if:
- D has previously been remanded in custody for the matter which is before the court;
- D is before the court;
- Both P and D have been allowed to make representations; and
- A date has been fixed for the next hearing and that hearing is expected to be effective (i.e. not solely relate to further remands).

D can be remanded in custody without being present in court if:
- D has consented to this at a previous hearing;
- D has a legal representative acting for him;
- D has not been remanded in absence on more than 2 consecutive occasions prior to the current one (i.e. **D can only be remanded in custody in his absence 3 times**);
- D has not withdrawn his earlier consent.

D can also be remanded in custody in his absence if he is unable to attend court due to illness or an accident. The remand will be until a convenient date.

The Custody Time Limit (CTL)

As at 31 December 2013 the Prosecution of Offences (Custody Time Limits) Regulations 1987 have not been amended to reflect the abolition of committals. The CTL which relates to offences committed to the Crown Court is now redundant.

The purpose of CTLs is to ensure that D is tried within a reasonable time. If the CTL expires D is entitled to be released on bail. Each offence for which D is charged attracts its own CTL.

D must not be kept in the custody of the Magistrates' Court for longer than:
- **70 days** if charged with an indictable offence (other than treason) or either-way offence which is sent[7] to the Crown Court.
- **70 days** if charged with an either-way offence which is to be tried summarily. However, **if the decision is made to try the case summarily within 56 days** of D's first appearance, the **time limit is reduced to 56 days.**
- **56 days** if charged with a summary offence.

---

[7] Reg 4 , Prosecution of Offences (Custody Time Limits) Regulations 1987 still refers to matters being committed to the Crown Court.

These time limits run from D's first appearance in the Magistrates' Court and cease on:
- The first day of D's trial in the Magistrates' Court; **or**
- The day D is sent to the Crown Court for trial.

When D is sent to the Crown Court for trial, the maximum period he can remain in custody is **182 days**, less the aggregate of any periods of time D was held in custody by the Magistrates' Court. The CTL runs from the date of being sent to the Crown Court and expires when the trial begins.

P can apply for an extension of the CTL, but this should only be granted if **BOTH**:[8]
- An extension is needed because:
  - D, the judge or a witness has been ill; or
  - The court has ordered separate trials for co-Ds and that causes a delay; or
  - Any other **good and sufficient cause**.
  AND
- P has acted **with all due diligence and expedition**.

3.3 The general right to bail under the Bail Act 1976 and the occasions when it does not apply

Under s.4 BA 1976, D enjoys a **general right to bail**. This is not an automatic right, but rather a presumption in favour of bail.

D has **no** general right to bail:
- When being arrested or charged;
- When a warrant for his arrest is issued;
- After conviction (unless the case is adjourned for reports to be made, or the conviction is for breaching a community order);
- When charged with an indictable offence and D was on bail at the time of the offence;
- When charged with homicide (= manslaughter or murder), rape or a serious sex offence **AND** D has a previous conviction for any of these. If so, the court is **required** to refuse bail except in **exceptional circumstances**.[9] Although note:
  - The homicide sentence D previously received must have been custodial;
  - For murder, bail will only be granted where there is **no significant risk that D will harm someone else** (burden on P to show that D will), and it **must** be a Crown Court judge that decides.[10] Magistrates can never grant bail in a murder case.

---

[8] s.22(3) POA 1985.
[9] s.25 CJPOA 1994.
[10] ss.114 and 115 Coroners and Justice Act 2009.

The grounds on which the court can refuse D bail vary depending on whether D is charged with:[11]

- An indictable only or an either-way imprisonable offence;
- A summary imprisonable offence or low value criminal damage;
- A non-imprisonable offence.

Many of these grounds overlap or are similar. The court has **eight** grounds available to it for the first category; **seven** for the second category; and **four** for the third.

1	2	3	
●			There are substantial grounds for believing that D will: ○ Fail to surrender (**FTS**) ○ Interfere with witnesses (**IWW**) ○ Commit further offences (**CFO**)
●			The offence is indictable only or either-way, and D was on bail at the time of the offence
●			A pre-sentence report must be written about D and this can only be done if D is in custody
●	●		D has tested positive for class A drugs and either: ○ D is charged with a drugs offence or an offence motivated/caused by D's drug habit; or ○ D has refused to undergo assessment or receive help.
●	●		The court has insufficient information, owing to a lack of time, to make an informed bail decision
●	●	●	D should be kept in custody for his own protection (or welfare, if a child)
●	●	●	D is already a serving prisoner
●	●	●	D had been granted bail in these proceedings but has been arrested for absconding or breaking bail conditions *[and for categories 2 and 3 only: **and** there are substantial grounds to believe that he will FTS, IWW or CFO]*
	●	●	D has previously failed to surrender AND the court believes he will fail to surrender again
	●		D was on bail at the time of the offence AND there are substantial grounds to believe that he would commit an offence if released
	●		There are substantial grounds for believing that D will commit an offence by engaging in conduct that will either cause physical or mental injury to another, or cause another to fear physical or mental injury

---

[11] See generally sch.1 to BA 1976.

By far the most common grounds on which a court will refuse bail are that D will **fail to surrender, commit further offences,** or **interfere with witnesses.**

Where D falls into the drugs provisions (fourth row in the table), the court is **required** to refuse bail **unless** there is no significant risk of him committing an offence whilst on bail.

In determining whether to refuse bail, the court should consider:[12]

> 1. The **nature and seriousness** of the offence, and the probable sentence.
> 2. D's **character, antecedents, associations and community ties.**
> 3. D's **record** of fulfilling bail conditions in the past.
> 4. The **strength of case** against D.

D has a right to hear the reasons for which he was refused bail.[13]

The strict rules of evidence do not apply to bail applications. D can give evidence in support of an application, and can be cross-examined.

3.5 Bail conditions that can be applied and under what circumstances

Unconditional Bail = D has a duty to surrender to the custody of the court at a given place and time, but no more.

Conditional Bail = D has the above duty **AND** has to comply with whatever conditions are laid down by the court.

The most common conditions are:
- Surety (= a person who promises to ensure D fulfils his bail conditions and promises a sum of money to the court. The money may be taken if D fails to surrender);
- Security (= a sum of money paid into court, which will not be returned if D fails to surrender);
- Reporting to the police station;
- Curfew (note: if D is placed under a 9 hour tagged curfew, half of these days will count towards a custodial sentence);
- Exclusion zone (= staying out of a certain area);
- Electronic tagging;
- Non-contact order.

---

[12] Para 9 sch.1 to BA 1976.
[13] s.5(3) BA 1976.

Bail conditions are virtually limitless: the judge will apply appropriate conditions to each individual D.

D has a right to hear the reasons for which conditions were imposed.[14]

Both D and P can apply to **vary** D's bail conditions, although advance notice of **24 hours and reasons** must be given.

3.6 The practice and procedure on appeal to the Crown Court against a decision to refuse bail in the Magistrates' Court

D can make up to **two bail applications** using the same arguments; after that D must show a change in circumstances or advance new considerations to reapply for bail.[15]

If bail is refused, the Magistrates must issue a certificate stating that they heard full argument.[16] This can be issued either after the first or second application (or subsequent application if there has been a change of circumstances). The certificate must state that the Magistrates heard full argument before refusing bail, and the change in circumstances that led them to rehear the application, if necessary.

D can then appeal to the Crown Court. The appeal takes the form of a bail application to a Crown Court judge.

D can also appeal against these bail conditions:[17]

- Residence requirement;
- Surety/security;
- Curfew;
- Tagging;
- Non-contact order.

D can only appeal against conditions when he has already applied to the Magistrates to vary them.

---

[14] s.5(3) BA 1976.
[15] s.154 CJA 1988.
[16] s.5(6A) BA 1976.
[17] s.16 CJA 2003.

3.7 The grounds upon which the prosecution can appeal to the Crown Court against a decision to grant bail

P can appeal the granting of bail when:
- D is charged with or convicted of an imprisonable offence; **and**
- The prosecution is brought by the CPS; **and**
- P objected to bail at the time it was granted.[18]

P must give oral notice of appeal **BEFORE** D is released from custody, followed by **written notice within 2 hours**, served on D and on the court. The appeal **must** be heard within 48 hours (not including weekends), and D will be kept in custody until then.

P can also ask for *"reconsideration"* of bail by the Magistrates, although only where:
- The offence is indictable only or either-way; **and**
- There is some information that was not available to the Magistrates originally.[19]

3.8 Dealing with defendants who have failed to surrender to bail or breached their bail conditions

Failing to surrender (FTS)

Failing to surrender to the custody of the court is an **offence under s.6 BA 1976**. The court will normally issue a warrant for D's arrest, and may take one or more of the following actions:
- Try D in his absence;
- Punish D for his failure to surrender;
- Remand D in custody or release him subject to more onerous conditions.

The **burden is on D** to bring and prove a reasonable excuse for failing to surrender if he wishes to avoid punishment; the standard of proof is the **balance of probabilities**.

Punishments available to the court for FTS are:
- Custody (3 months in the Magistrates' Court; 12 months in the Crown Court); **and/or**
- A Level 5 fine (= £5000 in Magistrates' Court, or unlimited in Crown Court).

The Magistrates can commit D to the Crown Court for sentence if necessary.

---

[18] s.1 Bail (Amendment) Act 1993.
[19] s.5B BA 1976.

The court can also order D to **forfeit his security** and/or order D's **surety to forfeit their recognizance** (= the sum of money promised to the court) in whole or in part.[20]

Other breach (e.g. of conditions)

Breach of any other bail condition is **not an offence under the BA 1976**, but will render D liable to arrest.[21] Police can arrest D:

- Where there are reasonable grounds to believe that D has or is about to break his bail conditions or fail to surrender;
- Where D's surety has informed the police that D is unlikely to surrender to custody and wishes to stop standing surety for D.

Once arrested, D will appear before the Magistrates within 24 hours, who will apply a two-stage test:

1.   Does one of the following apply?
- D has broken a bail condition;
- D was about to break a bail condition;
- D is likely not to surrender to custody.

2.   If not, grant D bail subject to the same conditions as before. But if so, consider future bail. The options are:[22]
- Remand/commit D to custody;
- Grant D bail on different conditions;
- Grant D bail on the same conditions.

---

[20] s.5(7) BA 1976 and s.120 MCA 1980.
[21] See generally s.7 BA 1976.
[22] s.7(5) BA 1976.

4. Plea in the Magistrates' Court, Mode of Trial, Allocation, Sending and Transfers

All cases start in a Magistrates' Court with D's **first appearance**. Then:
- For indictable-only matters, D will be **sent** to the Crown Court;
- For either-way matters, a plea will be taken from D and the case will be **allocated** to either the Crown Court or the Magistrates' Court;
- For summary matters, a plea will be taken from D and trial preparation will begin.

4.1 The rules relating to the provision of initial details[23]

Initial details   =   A **summary** of the P case, and/or any written statements or documents setting out the facts relied on, **and** a copy of D's previous convictions.

P must provide *"initial details"* of the P case as soon as practicable and no later than the beginning of the day of D's first appearance. It is usually provided at court on the day of D's first appearance in the Magistrates' Court.[24] Initial details allow D to make an informed decision on plea, and allocation if relevant.

4.2 Pleas generally in the Magistrates' Court, including equivocal pleas

A plea will be taken on the first appearance in summary only matters and an indication of plea is taken in either-way matters. Indictable only matters will be sent straight to the Crown Court from the first appearance, without a plea being taken.

In summary and either-way matters D can:
- Plead guilty;
- Plead not guilty;
- Make no indication as to plea.

An **equivocal plea** is a contradictory plea, i.e. where D pleads guilty but then immediately indicates his innocence. For example, to a rape charge, *"Guilty, but V was consenting"*. It is sometimes described as a *"guilty, but..."* plea. Where the plea is equivocal, the court will enter a not guilty plea on D's behalf.

The Magistrates have a discretion to allow D to change his plea at any time. If changed, they should also allow D to reconsider mode of trial.

---

[23] Formerly called *"advanced information"* and still regularly referred to by its old name (or acronym *"AI"*) in the Magistrates' Court.
[24] Normally initial details are also provided for indictable-only offences, but strictly there is no obligation to do so.

Where D is charged with an either-way offence and the Magistrates' Court accept jurisdiction, it becomes his choice whether to be tried in the Crown Court or the Magistrates' Court.

Magistrates' Court	Crown Court
Advantages	*Disadvantages*
• Less time to wait until trial (usually a matter of weeks) • Trial itself is usually shorter and quicker • More informal • Automatic right of appeal • Cheaper (remember: if D loses, he could be asked to pay P costs) • Magistrates' sentencing powers are more limited, but they can commit D to the Crown Court for sentence if necessary (see 22.1 below)	• Longer to wait until trial • Trial itself is longer • Crown Court proceedings are robed and more formal • No automatic right of appeal • Significantly more expensive • Crown Court sentencing powers are more extensive
Disadvantages	*Advantages*
• High conviction rate • No division between tribunal of fact and tribunal of law • Tribunal may be *"case-hardened"* • Lay bench is not legally trained	• Lower conviction rate: juries much more likely to acquit • Division between tribunal of fact and tribunal of law: minimal risk of tribunal of fact hearing inadmissible evidence • Jury unlikely to be *"case-hardened"* • Crown Court judge is familiar with hearing and ruling on complex legal arguments

Generally co-Ds both charged with an either-way offence can make separate decisions on mode of trial. (However, see 4.10 for instances when a co-D must be sent to the Crown Court).

The Magistrates only consider the question of jurisdiction where D is charged with an either-way offence (an indictable-only offence is sent to the Crown Court and summary offences stay in the Magistrates' Court).

The Magistrates will consider:
- The nature of the case;
- Whether the circumstances make the offence one of a serious character;
- Sentence, and whether their sentencing powers are sufficient.[25]

Cases likely to be declined by the Magistrates and sent to the Crown Court include those which are:
- Factually or legally complicated;
- Likely to be lengthy;
- Particularly serious or significant; or
- Likely to demand a serious sentence.

4.5 Plea before venue and allocation, including the special rules for criminal damage cases

Plea before venue

The charge is read to D. He *"indicates"* a plea:
- If *"Guilty"* the court will proceed as if D has actually pleaded guilty. Commit to Crown Court for sentencing if necessary;
- If *"Not Guilty"* the court will determine allocation (see below);
- If no indication is given, the court will treat this as a not guilty plea.

D should be present since he will indicate a plea. He will not be present only where:
- D is unruly **and** represented **and** it is not practicable to proceed in his presence and better to proceed in his absence; or
- There is a good reason for his absence (e.g. illness), **and** D is represented, **and** D consents; or
- D is in custody and present via live-link.

Allocation[26]

For either-way offences, once D has indicated a not guilty plea (or declined to indicate), the Magistrates must decide whether to accept jurisdiction, or decline jurisdiction and send the case to the Crown Court.

P will make representations on which venue is more appropriate. (Note that P can insist on a Crown Court trial if the DPP, Attorney General or Solicitor General brings the prosecution). D will then make representations if he wishes the trial to remain in the

---

[25] s.19(3) MCA 1980.
[26] Formerly called *"mode of trial"*.

Magistrates' Court. The Magistrates decide based on those representations (see 4.4), and they will assume that the P version of events is true.

There is a **general presumption in favour of summary trial.**

If D elected summary trial, he can apply to change to a Crown Court trial during his trial **with the Magistrates' consent.** The test is whether he understood the nature and significance of his choice.

The Magistrates can also decide to change to a Crown Court trial at **any time before the close of the P case** (e.g. where it becomes apparent that the offence is more serious than first realised).

Criminal damage

This is usually an either-way offence. However, if the damage is valued at **less than £5000 and did not involve fire** then it **MUST be treated as a summary offence** (and D cannot be committed for sentence). Note that:
- The value of the damage is market value at the time, not consequential loss;
- If the damage is more than £5000, it is an either-way offence;
- If the value is uncertain, then err on the side of summary jurisdiction;
- If there is more than one offence, the aggregate value will be used.

4.6 Committal for sentence

D can be committed to the Crown Court for sentence in 4 instances:

1.   The Magistrates have **insufficient sentencing powers.** This will be where:
- D is aged over 18; **and**
- He was convicted in the Magistrates' Court of an **either-way offence; and**
- The sentence needed is so serious that the Magistrates have insufficient powers.[27]

   The procedure should not normally be used **unless new information has come to light** since the allocation decision was taken. Also, where D has a **legitimate expectation** that he will be sentenced in the Magistrates' Court, he should not be committed for sentence.

2.   D pleads guilty to an either-way offence but is sent to the Crown Court for trial for a **related offence.**[28] If D is subsequently acquitted in the Crown Court then

---

[27] s.3 PCC(S)A 2000.
[28] s.4 PCC(S)A 2000.

sentencing powers of the judge in the Crown Court for the first offence are **limited to those of the Magistrates**.

3.   D is committed to the Crown Court for sentence under either of the provisions above, but still has to be sentenced for **other offences of which he has already been convicted, including summary offences.**[29] In dealing with these offences, the Crown Court judge's powers are limited to those of the Magistrates. This provision exists for convenience, to allow one court to deal with all outstanding matters.

4.   D **breaches a Crown Court Order** (i.e. a suspended sentence, community order or conditional discharge imposed by the Crown Court).

The Magistrates will warn D before trial that he could be committed for sentence. D can challenge a committal for sentence by way of judicial review (i.e. that the decision was *Wednesbury* unreasonable).

4.7 Sending either-way offences to the Crown Court for trial

The old procedure of committal to the Crown Court for trial (whereby the Magistrates' Court satisfied itself that there was sufficient evidence to put D on trial) has now been abolished. Where D is charged with an either-way matter and elects jury trial or jurisdiction is declined, the case is now **sent** to the Crown Court for trial.

4.8 Sending indictable only offences to the Crown Court

If D is over 18 and charged with an indictable-only offence, then the case is sent to the Crown Court immediately.[30] No plea is taken in the Magistrates' Court.

See 4.10 for when a related either-way or summary only offence might be tried in the Crown Court.

4.9 The transfer of complex fraud cases and cases involving child victims and witnesses (outline only)

The DPP and the Director of the Serious Fraud Office can give the Magistrates a notice of transfer, which transfers a case to the Crown Court. This can be used when:

- D has been charged with certain sexual offences or offences of violence or cruelty and a child will have to testify in the proceedings;[31] or

---

[29] s.6 PCC(S)A 2000. Note that the section refers to D being *"dealt with"* rather than *"sentenced"*.
[30] s.51 CDA 1998.

4.10 The sending of linked summary only (and either-way) cases and the procedure for dealing with them in the Crown Court

There are various scenarios in which summary only matters will be tried in the Crown Court, and in which either-way matters will be tried in the Crown Court without the usual allocation procedure applying.

Where a single D faces multiple charges

An either-way or summary offence may be sent to the Crown Court for trial where: [33]
- D is sent to the Crown Court for an indictable-only offence; **and**
- D also appears charged with an either-way or summary offence which appears to the court to be **related** to the offence for which he has been sent; **and**
- If a summary offence, it is punishable with either:
  - Imprisonment; **or**
  - Disqualification from driving.

The Magistrates:
- **Must** send the related either-way / summary offence to the Crown Court where D appears **on the same occasion** charged with both offences;
- **May** send the related either-way / summary offence where D has already been sent for an indictable-only and appears **on a subsequent occasion** charged with the related offence.

Where a summary offence is added to the indictment

If D has already been sent to the Crown Court for an indictable only offence, certain summary only offences can be **added to the indictment** by P without D having to re-appear in the Magistrates' Court for the case to be sent to the Crown Court.

This can happen where the summary offence was disclosed by the evidence on which D was sent for trial on indictment **and either:**
- It was founded on the same facts as the indictable offence; **or**
- It formed a series of offences of the same or similar character as the indictable offence.

These specific summary offences include: [34]
- Common assault;

---

[31] s.53 CJA 1991 and s.32(2) CJA 1988.
[32] s.4 CJA 1987.
[33] s.51(3) CDA 1998.
[34] s.40 CJA 1988.

- Criminal damage (less than £5000);
- Taking a motor vehicle without consent;
- Driving whilst disqualified.

Where there is an adult Co-D

Where D1 appears charged with an indictable only offence, and he and D2 are **jointly charged** with a **related either-way offence**, the Magistrates can not only send D1's either-way matter to the Crown Court (see above) but **can also send D2.**[35] This means that D2 will lose any opportunity to be tried in the Magistrates' Court.

The Magistrates:
- **Must** send D2's matter when he appears together with D1 **on the same occasion**;
- **May** send D2's matter when he appears on a **subsequent occasion**, after D1 has already been sent.

The Magistrates must also send D2 to the Crown Court for any other related charge which is:
- An either-way offence; **or**
- A summary offence which is punishable by imprisonment or disqualification from driving.

Where there is a youth Co-D

Youths will normally be tried summarily, in the Youth Court (even for indictable offences). However, where Youth-D is **jointly charged with an adult or is charged with a related offence,** and the adult matter is sent to the Crown Court, Youth-D **may** also be sent if it is **necessary in the interests of justice**. This applies whether Youth-D appears on the same or a subsequent occasion as adult-D, and whether adult-D is sent for an indictable only offence or for an either-way offence.[36]

Note that where this happens, the Magistrates **may** also send Youth-D to the Crown Court for any other **related** charge which is:
- An either-way offence; **or**
- A summary offence which is punishable by imprisonment or disqualification from driving.

---

[35] s.51(3) CDA 1998.
[36] See generally s.51 CDA 1998; s.46 CYPA 1933; and s.24A MCA 1980.

5. Disclosure of Unused Material and Defence Statements

5.1 The investigator's duty to retain unused material

The investigator **must retain material which may be relevant**, including:
- Crime reports;
- Custody records;
- Tapes;
- Witness statements;
- Interview records;
- Anything casting doubt on the reliability of other evidence.

Failure to retain this evidence may lead to a successful **abuse of process application by D**, on the grounds that he cannot have a fair trial or that it is otherwise unfair to try him.

5.2 The prosecutor's duty of disclosure

P must disclose to D all witness statements on which P relies, and anything which could be **reasonably considered capable of undermining the P case against D, or assisting D's case.**[37] This is an objective test.

5.3 The test for determining whether unused material should be disclosed by the prosecution, including the requirement of continuous review

Unused material to be disclosed will include anything that tends to show a fact inconsistent with the elements of the case that must be proved by P.

This includes:
- Anything that D would use in cross-examination, e.g. material that might:
  - Cast doubt upon accuracy of P evidence or the reliability of a P witness;
  - Suggest that someone else committed the offence;
  - Suggest that D's confession is unreliable;
  - Support D's defence or alibi.
- Anything that D would use to persuade the court to:
  - Exclude evidence;
  - Stay proceedings;
  - Make a declaration of incompatibility with D's ECHR rights.
- Anything that suggests an explanation or partial explanation of D's actions.

---

[37] s.3 CPIA 1996.

P must inform D if any P witnesses have previous convictions, if these pass the disclosure test.

There is a **continuing duty to disclose**. This means that where P comes into possession of, or belatedly realises that he has possession of, relevant material, it must be disclosed immediately.

Only material whose **disclosure would not be in the public interest is exempt** from these disclosure rules (see 5.9 below).

5.4 Time limits for prosecution disclosure

P must provide *"initial details"* of the P case as soon as practicable and no later than the beginning of the day of D's first appearance. It is usually provided at court on the day of D's first appearance in the Magistrates' Court.[38]

Initial details = A **summary** of the P case, and/or any written statements or documents setting out the facts relied on, **and** a copy of D's previous convictions.

Where D is to be tried summarily, the Magistrates' Court standard directions set out that P must serve all of the evidence on which it intends to rely upon at trial **within 28 days of D's plea**. If D is sent for trial at the Crown Court, P must disclose to D the evidence it will rely upon at trial **within 50 days of sending if D is in custody or within 70 days if D is on bail**.

There is **no statutory time-limit for the disclosure of unused material**. Such material **should be disclosed as soon as reasonably practicable**. However, the courts will frequently direct that any unused material is disclosed at the same time as P serves the evidence on which it will rely at trial.

5.5 Applications to compel the prosecution to disclose

After P has received D's defence statement, P must either:
- Disclose more material, e.g. material relevant to the issues raised by D, or material requested by D, in his defence statement; or
- Give a written statement that P has no further relevant material.

If D has **reasonable grounds to believe** that P still has relevant material which has not been disclosed, **D can apply to force disclosure**.[39] An application to compel P to disclose must outline in writing:

---

[38] Normally initial details are provided for indictable-only offences, but strictly there is no obligation to do so.

- The material sought;
- Why D thinks P has it;
- Why it is necessary to disclose;
- Why a hearing is needed, if relevant.

D should serve the application on P and the court; P can make representations to the court immediately or within 14 days.

5.6 Defence duties of disclosure

D **must** supply a defence statement in the Crown Court; he **may** supply one in the Magistrates' Court.

D should serve his defence statement:
- In the **Magistrates' Court, within 14 days** of P complying with his initial duty to disclose;
- In the **Crown Court, within 28 days** of P complying with his initial duty to disclose.

The court may extend this deadline, on application by D, and only if it is unreasonable to expect D serve a defence statement by then.

5.7 The requirements relating to the contents of a defence statement

A defence statement should set out **ALL** of:
- The nature of the defence, including any particular defences on which D relies;
- Any points of law D wishes to take;
- For each issue, why D takes issue with P;
- Whether D wishes to call witnesses, and if so their name, address and date of birth;
- If D gives an alibi: the name, address and date of birth of the alibi witness;
- The name of any experts instructed, even those not called as witnesses.

The court **may** require D to serve his defence statement on co-Ds.

5.8 The consequences of defence failures in the disclosure process

Failure to provide a defence statement (in the Crown Court), or departing from the defence statement at trial (in both the Magistrates' Court and the Crown Court) means

---

[39] s.8 CPIA 1996.

that an **adverse inference may be drawn, and any other party (including the court) can comment on it** (although see below).

Departure from the defence statement includes advancing an unmentioned alibi, running a different defence, or relying on key facts not mentioned.

If D failed in his defence statement to mention a point of law or failed to include a witness, the permission of the court is needed before P (or any other party) can comment on it.

D never loses his right to P disclosure or his right to call a particular witness.

5.9 Public interest immunity and public policy

P can withhold material on the basis of **public interest immunity** (PII) with the **permission of the court**. PII will apply when disclosure would **risk serious prejudice to an important public interest**.

This includes material which:
- Relates to national security;
- Has been received from intelligence agencies;
- Might facilitate the commission of a crime;
- Reveals the identity of an informant;
- Reveals the location of a police surveillance point.[40]

This list is not exhaustive.

There are **3** general ways the application may be made:
- P gives notice to D that P will make a PII application, and states on which broad grounds. D can then make submissions opposing the application.

- P gives notice to D that P will make a PII application, but does not state on which broad grounds. D can make submissions about procedure, but the application itself will be without D or his representative.

- The application is totally *ex parte*. P gives no notice and D does not even know the application ever happened. P must explain to the court why this is necessary. The court can appoint **special counsel** for the D, i.e. an independent barrister who acts on D's behalf but does not reveal anything to D.

---

[40] See generally Part II CPIA 1996.

The test in a PII application comes from _R v H_:[41]

1. Is there a real risk of serious prejudice to an important public interest if full disclosure is ordered?
2. Can D's interests be protected without disclosure or with partial disclosure?
3. Is this the minimum necessary to protect the public interest?
4. Will this render the whole trial unfair?

5.10 Third party disclosure

Sometimes relevant evidence is in the hands of a third party (i.e. someone who is neither D nor P). P's duty of disclosure extends to pursuing all reasonable lines of enquiry, and either obtaining any resulting evidence from the third party or inviting the third party to retain it in case D seeks disclosure. Failure to do this might lead to the proceedings being **stayed as an abuse of process**.

The third party may disclose the material **voluntarily**. However, if they refuse to do so they can be **compelled to disclose** it.[42] Both P and D can apply for compulsory disclosure; the test is that:

- The third party is likely to be able to give or produce material evidence in the case; **and**
- The third party will not voluntarily attend or voluntarily produce the evidence.

The application must be made orally or in writing **as soon as practicable** after becoming aware of the grounds for doing so. The third party can object at a hearing and put forward any reasons why compulsory disclosure should not be ordered.

If the application is successful, a **witness summons will be issued** compelling the third party to attend court with the relevant evidence or to disclose the evidence in advance.

---

[41] [2004] 2 AC 134.
[42] See generally CrimPR rule 28.

6. The Indictment

6.1 The time limits for preferring a bill of indictment

An indictment is a written accusation of crime made by P against D.

P must serve the draft indictment on the Crown Court officer **not more than 28 days** after:
- D has been committed or transferred for trial;
- Service of a notice of transfer (see 4.9 above);
- Copies of the documents containing the evidence against D have been served on the Crown Court and D (where D has been sent for trial);
- A High Court judge has given permission to serve the indictment;
- The Court of Appeal orders a retrial.

The Crown Court may extend this time limit, even after it has expired.

The Crown Court officer will date and sign the indictment upon receipt, and then serve it upon all parties. The CrimPR require that the indictment be signed and dated, but this is **not** a statutory requirement.

6.2 The structure and format of an indictment

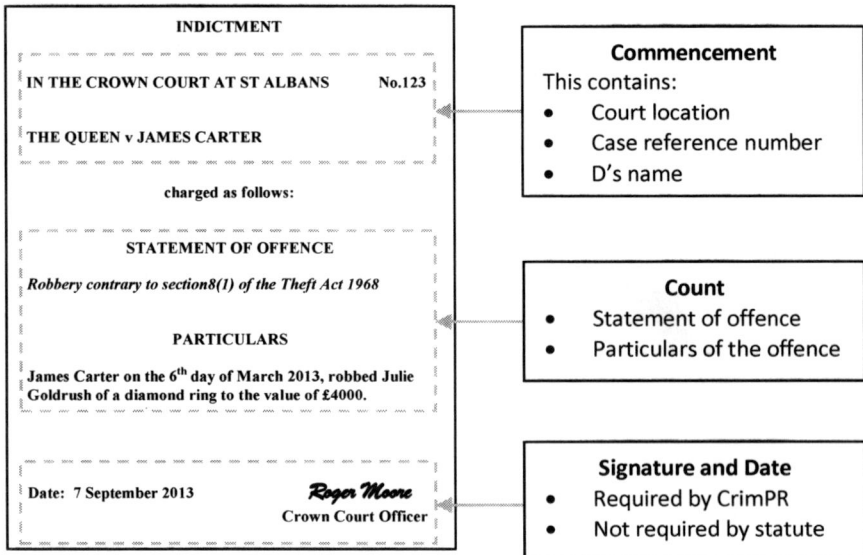

INDICTMENT

IN THE CROWN COURT AT ST ALBANS   No.123

THE QUEEN v JAMES CARTER

charged as follows:

STATEMENT OF OFFENCE

Robbery contrary to section8(1) of the Theft Act 1968

PARTICULARS

James Carter on the 6th day of March 2013, robbed Julie Goldrush of a diamond ring to the value of £4000.

Date: 7 September 2013   *Roger Moore*
                                 Crown Court Officer

Commencement
This contains:
- Court location
- Case reference number
- D's name

Count
- Statement of offence
- Particulars of the offence

Signature and Date
- Required by CrimPR
- Not required by statute

6.3 The format of a count

Each count is divided into 2 parts:
- The **Statement of Offence**, which describes the offence and identifies any creating statute;
- The **Particulars of Offence**, which contain the facts of the charge and detail the essential elements of the offence.

6.4 Counts which can be lawfully joined on an indictment

An indictment:
- **Must** contain counts which are substantially the same as the offences for which D has been sent for trial;
- **May** contain any count based on the evidence served and triable in the Crown Court.

An indictment may contain multiple counts if:
- Each count is **founded on the same set of facts**. There must be a common factual origin e.g.:
  - The offences occurred in the same incident;
  - One offence could not have occurred, unless the other had already been committed.

or

- The counts form or are part of a **series of offences which are similar in nature**, e.g. a string of burglaries.

For details of summary offences which may be included on an indictment see 4.10.

6.5 The rules relating to duplicity, specimen counts and overloading

Duplicity

No single count should charge D with two or more separate offences. If it does, it is said to be **bad for duplicity**. However, a count may contain multiple incidents if those incidents amount to a **single course of conduct** in relation to time, place or purpose.[43]

If statute creates a single offence which may be committed in more than one way, it is acceptable to include all the ways in which the offence was committed in a single count. However, if the statute creates more than one offence then there must be a separate count for each offence.

---

[43] CrimPR rule 14.2.

If a count is bad for duplicity D may apply to have it quashed, but normally P will be permitted to amend it.

Specimen counts

Where the evidence reveals that D committed a large number of offences in a systematic manner, it is sometimes not appropriate or not possible to include a count for all. Instead, sample counts will be used, called specimen counts. This method is generally used when:

- P is **unable to supply particulars** of all the offences committed by D, perhaps because V alleges criminality against him on many occasions and cannot give precise details of each one. P will allege a single offence of each type committed in the relevant time period, and will rely on *"course of conduct"* evidence to prove it; or
- P can supply particulars of all offences but they are **so numerous and similar** that it would render a trial unworkable. P will choose a small number of sample offences which represent the whole.

Specimen counts are often used in sexual abuse cases and in complex financial cases involving many transactions.

If specimen counts are used, D must know the case he has to meet. So P should provide:

- A list of all the offences D is alleged to have committed and from which the specimen counts have been selected; **and**
- Evidence of the other offences, if appropriate.

D may only be sentenced on the basis of the counts of which he has been convicted (or which he admits); to do otherwise would deny him his right to a trial. For this reason, enough specimen counts should be used to reflect the full criminality of D.

Overloading

P has a duty not to overload the indictment with too many charges and/or Ds. Even if it is technically permissible to include all of the counts in a single indictment, P should use a number of shorter indictments if a single indictment will:

- Result in an unduly long or complicated trial;
- Place an unfair burden on the jury;
- Not be in the interests of justice.

In complicated cases P may be required to identify the counts on which it will proceed to trial and leave the rest to **lie on the file** (see 7.4). This is most common in cases of conspiracy and complex fraud.

If P has overloaded the indictment, the court has the power to intervene of its own accord and order separate trials.

6.6 The joinder of defendants on an indictment

It is possible to have multiple Ds on an indictment if:
- All Ds participated in the same offence; **or**
- Although the Ds are not charged with the same offence, the offences are sufficiently linked to be joined.

6.7 Applications to sever the indictment

The court has the power to sever an indictment and order separate trials for specific counts. This power can only be used if the counts are properly joined on the original indictment: it cannot be used to remedy misjoinder.

Typically the application to sever will be made by a D who faces multiple counts and who seeks separate trials for separate offences, or by co-Ds in a multi-D trial who seek to be tried separately.

The normal position is that **counts properly joined will be tried together**. The discretion to sever will only be exercised if:
- A single trial would prejudice or embarrass D in the conduct of his defence;
- It is desirable for some other reason.[44]

There is a presumption in favour of a joint trial for multiple Ds because this avoids:
- The risk of inconsistent verdicts;
- Witnesses having to give the same evidence on multiple occasions;
- The expense of multiple trials.

If multiple Ds wish to have separate trials it is necessary for them to show that there is no chance of a fair trial otherwise.

6.8 The consequences of misjoinder

If an indictment has been misjoined (= counts have been incorrectly joined on one indictment), there is **no power to sever it** and hold separate trials.

The situation can only be rectified by:
- Deleting counts as required, so that the indictment only contains properly joined counts;
- Staying the misjoined indictment and P serving new indictments which are properly joined.

---

[44] s.5(3) Indictments Act 1915.

Misjoinder does not nullify the whole indictment. Therefore if D challenges a misjoined indictment, only the wrongly joined counts will be quashed.

6.9 Applications to amend indictments

An application to amend a defective indictment can be made before or at any stage of trial, provided this will not cause injustice.

Amendments can include:
- Adding new Ds;
- Adding new counts;
- Substituting new counts for existing ones.

6.10 Applications to quash and stay indictments

An **application to quash an indictment** (quash = annul) is the most common means of challenging a defective indictment. It is normally made before D has pleaded to the indictment, and can be made by either P or D. The indictment will be quashed if the application is well founded and there is **no means of correcting the defect**. P can normally defeat a D application to quash the indictment simply by amending it so that it is correct.

An **application to stay an indictment** (stay = postpone or suspend, usually indefinitely) is generally used when there is nothing procedurally wrong with the indictment itself, but D alleges that it is an abuse of process.

In certain circumstances the indictment may be challenged by judicial review of the underlying sending or committal.

6.11 Voluntary bills of indictment (outline only)

Voluntary bill of indictment = bill of indictment preferred on the direction of, or with the consent of, a judge of the High Court.[45]

A voluntary bill of indictment is an alternative to the usual route of being sent to the Crown Court by the Magistrates' Court. Consent will be granted by the High Court judge only *exceptionally*, and only where **good reason can be shown to depart from the usual** procedure.

---

[45] s.2(2)(b) of the Administration of Justice (Miscellaneous Provisions) Act 1933. For the application procedure see the Indictments Procedure Rules 1971.

This route might be used when, for example, there is an incurable defect in the indictment or a defect in the sending procedure, such that proceedings cannot continue.

7. Preliminaries to Trial in the Crown Court

7.1 The plea and case management hearing in the Crown Court and its importance to case management

With the introduction of the early guilty plea scheme, in general the first hearing in the Crown Court will now be a preliminary hearing or an early guilty plea hearing (see 7.5).

Furthermore, there **must** be a Plea and Case Management Hearing (PCMH) at the Crown Court in every case, unless the circumstances make it unnecessary. Where there is no early guilty plea hearing or preliminary hearing the PCMH should be held:
- Within about **13 weeks** of sending for trial where D is in custody; **or**
- Within about **16 weeks** of sending if D is on bail.

The broad purpose of holding a PCMH is to prevent trials being delayed, cracked or ineffective by ensuring that timetables are being followed and issues which may affect trial are raised well in advance of the trial date.

Before the hearing all parties will fill in a standard PCMH form and give it to the judge. Issues to be considered at a PCMH (and/or covered by the PCMH form) include:
- Plea;
- Service of P evidence;
- Disclosure required by D;
- Defence statement;
- Expert evidence;
- Witnesses to be called;
- Whether any admissions can be made and evidence agreed;
- Special measures needed to assist D or another witness;
- Bad character/hearsay;
- The admissibility of evidence;
- Public interest immunity.

The judge will engage in **active case management**, and can direct the parties to carry out any steps necessary to ensure the smooth and timely running of the trial.

7.2 Arraignment

Arraignment = the formal process of asking D whether he pleads guilty or not guilty.

Arraignment is carried out in open court by the court clerk, who:
- Identifies D by name; then
- Reads the indictment to D; then

- Asks D whether he pleads guilty or not guilty.

If there are multiple counts on the indictment, a plea must be taken following each count, before reading out the next count. If there are multiple Ds, they are often arraigned together but must offer separate pleas.

D must plead personally: his advocate cannot plead on his behalf.

The arraignment usually takes place at an early guilty plea hearing if D has indicated that he intends to plead guilty, or at the PCMH if D has indicated a not guilty plea.

7.3 Special pleas, autrefois acquit and convict (outline only)

A *special plea in bar* is a plea by which the defendant claims that it would be unlawful to try him. There are four special pleas:
- Autrefois acquit;
- Autrefois convict;
- Pardon;
- Special liability of another to make repairs (of historical relevance only).

Autrefois acquit = literally, "formerly acquitted". D claims that he has previously been tried and acquitted of the offence.

Autrefois convict = literally, "formerly convicted". D claims that he has previously been tried and convicted of the offence.

Pardon = D claims to have received a pardon in relation to this offence.

It would infringe the principle against **double jeopardy** to try D for an offence of which he has previously been acquitted or convicted, or for a very similar offence arising out of the same facts; there is a substantial body of case law concerning the pleas of autrefois acquit and autrefois convict and when they might apply. Where the court finds in D's favour, the prosecution will be stayed.

7.4 Pleas to alternative counts, offering no evidence and leaving counts to lie on file

Alternative counts

In certain situations, D can also plead guilty to an alternative offence.

This can be:

- Where an alternative count appears on the indictment. This is a count that is **mutually inconsistent with another count**, so that P alleges that D is guilty of either one count or of the other, **but not both**. The court cannot convict D of both;
- An express or implied alternative, i.e. where:
  - **If words were deleted** from the description of the main offence on the indictment the result would be **the description of the lesser offence** (e.g. *"causing grievous bodily harm with intent"* >> *"causing grievous bodily harm"*); or
  - The **lesser offence is a necessary step** towards the commission of the main offence (e.g. *"dangerous driving"* >> *"careless driving"*).

Where the alternative count appears on the indictment, D will be asked to plead to the more serious count first, and only if he pleads not guilty will the lesser count be put to him. Where the alternative count is express or implied but is not a separate count on the indictment, D can of his own accord offer a guilty plea to the lesser alternative. P will then decide whether to accept the plea to the alternative.

If P accepts the plea to the alternative, D is formally acquitted of the other offence.

For example:

> 1. D has been caught on the street of a burglary with stolen goods. He is charged on an indictment with two counts: one count of burglary, and an alternative count of handling stolen goods. On P's case, D was **either** the burglar, **or** he received the goods from the burglar. D could offer a guilty plea to either alternative count.
>
> 2. D is charged on an indictment with a single count of attempted murder (for which the mens rea is an intention to kill). He could offer a plea of guilty to the implied alternative offence of causing grievous bodily harm with intent (for which the mens rea is an intention to cause really serious harm).

Offering no evidence

Offering no evidence at trial is a course taken by P as an alternative to discontinuing a prosecution (generally because the need to discontinue arises on the day of trial). P can offer no evidence at any time until the close of the P case.

Where P offers no evidence, D is formally acquitted. P cannot then bring another prosecution against D for the same offence, as this would breach the principle against double jeopardy. Note that offering no evidence is **not** the same as dropping a charge (where a charge is dropped, action ceases against D but he is not formally acquitted. It is open to P to bring fresh charges against D).

Leaving counts to lie on the file

Leaving a count to lie on the file means that no further action can be taken against D on that count without the leave of the court. However, D is not acquitted or convicted, and in theory the count can be resurrected.

P needs to ask the **permission of the court** to leave counts to lie on the file.

7.5 Preliminary and pre-trial hearings in complex and serious and sensitive cases, including the powers of dismissal of transferred and sent cases

In most instances the first hearing in the Crown Court will now be an early guilty plea hearing or a preliminary hearing.

Early guilty plea hearing

The Magistrates' Court or Crown Court may order an early guilty plea hearing where it is anticipated that D will plead guilty. The aim of such hearings is to allow the case to be dealt with promptly.

D will normally be arraigned and sentenced at this hearing and so parties must be adequately prepared. This will include:
- Being able to address any issues relating to a basis of plea;
- Ensuring a pre-sentence report has been prepared if necessary;
- Obtaining medical and/or any other material required for sentencing; and
- Quantifying costs.

The arrangement for scheduling early guilty plea hearings varies between criminal justice areas, depending on the directions given by the presiding judges. Within London, for example, the early guilty plea hearing will take place within 10-14 days of the matter being sent to the Crown Court if no pre-sentence report is required and within 4 weeks of sending if a report is needed.

Preliminary hearings

If an early guilty plea hearing is not ordered, normally a preliminary hearing will be held. Although such hearings are held as standard, note that they should be ordered if:
- Case management issues make it necessary;
- The trial estimate is more than 4 weeks;
- An early trial date is desirable; or

- D is a child or young person.

The preliminary hearing should take place **14-21 days after the matter has been sent for trial.**

The aim of the preliminary hearing is to allow the Crown Court actively to manage the case from an early stage, by setting timetables and giving clear directions. Matters the court will consider at the hearing include:
- Any guilty pleas offered;
- Setting the date for the PCMH and trial; and
- Any bail applications.

Preparatory hearings

A preparatory hearing is a pre-trial hearing ordered by a Crown Court judge in certain cases, held **after the PCMH but before trial**. Its purpose is generally to finalise how the evidence will be presented to the jury to ensure that they can understand and follow it, and to address any other issues which may affect the running of the trial. Questions of admissibility, law and severance and joinder can also be addressed.[46]

The judge **may** order a preparatory hearing where:
- He feels that the case is of **such complexity, seriousness or length** that a hearing is needed before trial; **or**
- There will be an application to hold **a trial without a jury** (see 9.1 below).

The judge **must** order a preparatory hearing where any of the counts is a **terrorism** offence, or has a terrorist connection and is punishable by 10 years' imprisonment or more.

Both P and D can make an application for a preparatory hearing to be held, or the judge can order one of his own motion.

Applications for dismissal

D may apply for any charge against him to be dismissed if the evidence against him is not sufficient for him properly to be convicted. The application can be made orally or in writing, but must be made:
- After D has been served with the evidence on which the charge is based; **but**
- Before D has been arraigned.

On such an application the judge must dismiss the charge if the evidence against D is not sufficient for him properly to be convicted.

---

[46] ss.7-10 CJA1987 and ss.29-34 CPIA 1996.

Section 3

Issues relating to criminal trials

8. Summary Trial Procedure

8.1 Circumstances in which the Magistrates can proceed in the absence of the defendant

The Magistrates can proceed in the absence of D in any of these 3 instances:

1. Where D fails to attend court

If D is **over 18** the Magistrates **must** hear the case in D's absence, unless it is contrary to the interests of justice. If D is **under 18** the Magistrates **may** proceed in his absence. The court must not proceed with the trial if there is an acceptable reason for D's absence although there is no obligation on the Magistrates to enquire as to the reason.

If the trial does proceed, a not guilty plea will be entered on D's behalf.

For an either-way offence, the trial can only proceed if D was present previously to consent to summary trial.

If proceedings began by means of charge and requisition (or laying an information and summons), **P must prove that the charge and requisition/summons was served on D.** Proof of postage is sufficient.

If D did not know of the proceedings, he may make a **statutory declaration** of this fact,[47] which will **render the trial and conviction void**. The declaration must be made **within 21 days** of D becoming aware of the proceedings and is likely to be followed by a retrial.

2. Where D pleads guilty by post

D can plead guilty by sending a letter to the court where he is:
- Accused of a **summary offence**; and
- Proceedings were **commenced by a summons or charge and requisition**.

P must have served all of the following on D and notified this fact to the court:
- Summons or charge and requisition;
- Statement of the facts on which P relies or the witness statements;
- Any information about D that may be put before the court;
- A notice explaining the process for pleading by post.

D may include with his postal plea a statement detailing any mitigation. D has the right to withdraw this plea before the hearing, and may be allowed to so at the hearing.

---

[47] s.142 MCA 1980.

If D has pleaded guilty by post, neither P nor D will be represented at court. The statements on which the charge is based must be read out by the clerk in open court, or the resulting conviction will be quashed.

The Magistrates can then **sentence in D's absence or adjourn for D to be present**. However, they cannot impose a custodial sentence or a disqualification in his absence.[48]

3. Where D is disorderly

If D behaves in such a manner that the proceedings cannot continue, he will be removed from the court and the trial will continue. D is considered to be present if he has legal representation, unless statute requires his physical presence.

8.2 Abuse of process in the Magistrates' Court (outline only)

The Magistrates' Court has the power to stay a prosecution as an abuse of the process of the court where it will be impossible to give D a fair trial. This is a narrower power than that enjoyed by the Crown Court (see 9.3 below).

Factors that may render it impossible to try D fairly include e.g.:
* Disclosure failures by P;
* Adverse media publicity;
* Where key evidence is unavailable to D to examine;
* Delay in charging D.

The power to stay proceedings should be exercised most sparingly. The decision of the Magistrates' Court can be challenged in the High Court by way of judicial review.

When D applies for a stay in the Magistrates' Court on the grounds that his trial amounts to a misuse or manipulation of the process of the court (see 9.3 below), the Magistrates have no jurisdiction to hear the issue, and must adjourn proceedings and allow the application to be made to the High Court.

8.3 The procedural steps in a summary trial

A summary trial will proceed as follows:

1. The **plea**, which must be unequivocal.

2. **P's opening speech**, outlining the P case against D (see 8.5).

---

[48] s.11 MCA 1980.

3.   **The Prosecution case**: P's evidence proving the allegation against D (e.g. live witnesses; agreed statements that are read out (s.9 CJA 1967); admitted facts that are written down and read out (s.10 CJA 1967); D's interview summary, etc). See 9.5 for more details.

4.   **(Submission of no case to answer** at the close of the P case if D chooses to make one – see 8.4).

5.   **Explanation to D**. The court or its legal adviser should explain all of the following:
      • That D has the right to give evidence;
      • The consequences of not giving evidence;
      • The consequences of not answering a question while giving evidence.

6.   **The Defence case**: evidence in a similar fashion to the P case. D will testify before any other live witness. Remember the burden of proof: D is not obliged to call evidence, testify or in any way prove his case.

7.   **Additional evidence,** if any. After the defence evidence, either party may adduce further evidence if it is admissible (e.g. rebuttal evidence).

8.   **Closing Speeches**. See 8.5.

9.   **Verdict**. See 8.6.

10.   **Sentence**, if D is convicted. The judge will hear D's **antecedents** (= previous convictions). Sentencing may occur after an adjournment, if there is a need to prepare additional information such as a pre-sentence report, or for some other reason. Before being sentenced, D may make a **plea in mitigation**, outlining why the judge should pass a lenient sentence, before the judge makes his sentencing decision.

8.4 Submission of no case to answer

At the end of the P case the court may acquit D on the grounds that P's evidence is **insufficient for any reasonable court properly to convict**. This may be on the application of D (who makes a **submission of no case to answer**), or by the court of its own initiative. See 9.5 for more details.

P **must** be allowed to make submissions before D can be acquitted on these grounds. The court may also allow P to re-open its case to supply sufficient evidence.

The Magistrates **need not give reasons for rejecting** a submission of no case to answer. Where the submission is rejected, the trial continues to the D case as normal.

8.5 Order of the speeches

Opening speeches

P has the right to make an opening speech, which will happen at the start of P's case. The opening speech will outline the facts of the allegation and make reference to the evidence which will be called, usually including a summary of D's police interview.

D has no right to make an opening speech in a summary trial. D's case normally begins by calling evidence immediately.

Closing speeches

P may only make a closing speech if:
- D is legally represented; **or**
- D has called witnesses of fact other than himself.

Where P makes a closing speech, it will be made **before** the D closing speech. In many summary trials, especially those that are straightforward and short, P will make no speech even where entitled to.

D makes a closing speech after P. If there are multiple Ds, the speeches will be in the order the Ds are listed on the information.

8.6 Verdicts

A district judge will usually give the verdict immediately upon the conclusion of speeches, whereas lay Magistrates retire (without the legal adviser) to consider the verdict.

The verdict of a lay bench **must be a majority** decision. The bench will usually comprise 3 members, but can sit with a minimum of 2. In the event of a bench of 2 being evenly split:
- The chair **does not** have a casting vote; and
- There must be a **fresh trial in front of a new bench** of Magistrates.

If D is convicted the Magistrates **must give sufficient reasons** to explain the decision. This is not necessary if D is acquitted.

Unlike a jury, the Magistrates have **no power to find D guilty of an alternative offence** not specifically charged, although there are some statutory exceptions to this. However, in a summary trial P may prefer 2 charges in the alternative from the beginning.

The court may make an order for D's costs to be paid out of central funds (a "defendant's costs order") if, for example, any of the below apply:[49]

- An information laid before the court was not proceeded with;
- The court dismisses an information;
- D is sent for trial but then not tried;
- D is tried on indictment and acquitted;
- D successfully appeals a Magistrates' Court conviction or sentence in the Crown Court;
- D successfully appeals a Crown Court conviction in the court of appeal.

It is in the court's discretion whether to award costs depending on the circumstances of the case. Costs awarded will cover any expenses "properly incurred"; where the court considers it inappropriate to award full costs, D will be awarded a "just and reasonable" sum.

Under LASPO 2012, defendant's costs orders are limited to legal aid rates. Moreover, those who seek private representation in the Crown Court will not be entitled to a defendant's costs order at all.

If D is convicted, P costs can be awarded against D if the court is satisfied D has the means to pay. The order is not intended to be in the nature of a penalty.

The court can also order costs against any party which have been incurred as a result of an **unnecessary or improper act or omission** by that party. The court also has the power to order a legal or other representative of the party to meet the whole or part of the wasted costs.[50]

The legal adviser gives lay Magistrates any legal advice they need to carry out their role. The advice may be given whether requested or not. The legal adviser **must not** play any part in the finding of fact.

The legal adviser will advise on:

- Questions of law;
- Questions of mixed law and fact;
- Practice and procedure;
- The penalties available;
- Relevant guidelines and/or authorities.

---

[49] s.16 POA 1985.
[50] s.19(1) POA 1985.

The legal adviser may also assist the Magistrates by reminding them of the evidence, and with the formulation of reasons for decisions.

9. Jury Trial Procedure

9.1 Judge only trials (outline only)

A trial can be conducted by judge alone in two instances:[51]
- *Where there is a real and present danger of **jury tampering**;*
- *In **complex fraud** trials (not in force as of 31 December 2013).*[52]

Trial by judge alone must be in the interests of justice. Examples of when there may be a real and present danger of jury tampering include:
- *In a retrial where the jury in the original trial was discharged because of jury tampering;*
- *Jury tampering has taken place in any previous proceedings involving any of the Ds;*
- *Where there has been intimidation or attempted intimidation of any likely witness.*

In addition, a judge may try alone some, but not all, of the counts on the indictment if the following conditions are met:
- *The number of counts means that trial by jury involving all of the counts would be impracticable; and*
- *Each count or group of counts tried with the jury can be regarded as a sample of counts which could be tried without the jury; and*
- *It is in the interests of justice.*[53]

9.2 Proceeding in the absence of the defendant

If D is absent on any date fixed for trial the judge **has the discretion to start or continue the trial without D.** In addition, if it appears that D has absconded, a **bench warrant will be issued** for his arrest.

In deciding whether to continue in the absence of D all circumstances should be considered, including e.g.:
- The nature and circumstance of D's absence and whether the absence is voluntary;
- Whether an adjournment would resolve the situation and the likely length of any such adjournment;
- Whether D wanted or waived representation;
- If D's representatives have or could take instructions;

---

[51] ss.43-44 CJA 2003.
[52] s.43 CJA 2003 has been repealed, but the repeal cannot take effect until s.43 CJA 2003 has been brought into force.
[53] s.17 Domestic Violence, Crime and Victims Act 2004.

- The extent of the disadvantage to D, because he will not be able to present his account;
- The risk of the jury reaching an improper conclusion because of the absence;
- The public interest in the trial taking place in reasonable time;
- The effect of delay on the memory of the witnesses;
- The undesirable nature of separate trials for multiple Ds.

9.3 Abuse of process in the Crown Court (Outline Only)

The court has an inherent power to protect its process from abuse by staying an indictment, where either:

- It will be **impossible to give D a fair trial**, e.g. because of:
    - Disclosure failures by P;
    - Adverse media publicity;
    - Key evidence being unavailable to D to examine;
    - Delay in charging D; or

- The proceedings amount to a misuse or manipulation of the court's process, because it would **offend the court's sense of justice and** propriety to try D in the circumstances of the particular case.

Written notice must be given of any application to stay the indictment as an abuse of process. The trial judge will determine the matter, considering any material provided by P and D. The **burden of proof is on D** and the standard is the **balance of probabilities**.

An order that all of part of the indictment should be stayed cannot be challenged by way of judicial review. An appeal against the decision of the trial judge lies to the Court of Appeal.

9.4 The law and practice relating to juries

Serving on a jury

Any person can serve on a jury unless he is:
- Mentally disordered; **or**
- Disqualified because he:
    - Is on **bail** at the time of the jury service; or
    - Has **ever** had a **custodial sentence** in the UK of **5 years or more**; or
    - In the **last 10 years has had any custodial sentence or suspended** custodial sentence in the UK; or
    - In the **last 10 years has had a community order** in England and Wales.

A juror should stand down if an impartial observer would conclude on the facts that the juror has an appearance of bias, e.g. a juror should stand down if:
- He knows D or a witness;
- He is employed by the CPS and is sitting on a trial being prosecuted by that agency;
- He is a police officer and knows or is connected with the police officers involved in the case.

There is no entitlement to refuse to do jury service, but it is possible to seek a deferral or to be excused.

Empanelling the jury

A number of potential jurors (normally 15) will be brought into court. The court clerk will read out 12 randomly selected names of those present. D will be informed that he has the right to **challenge the empanelling of a juror** before the juror is sworn in.

There are two ways to challenge a juror:

1. **Standby** (available to **P only**). There is no need for P to give its reasons. Used when the juror is:
   - Deemed unsuitable in circumstances where the jury has been vetted;
   - Manifestly unsuitable for the type of trial that is to be conducted.

   The challenge is made by the prosecutor saying *"standby"* just as the juror's oath starts. The judge also has this power but will rarely exercise it. Any person subject to this challenge **cannot** sit on the jury, but may be required for another jury. It is not appropriate to use standby to achieve a racially balanced jury.

2. **Challenge for cause** (available to **both D and P**). Used when the potential juror is **suspected of bias**. No questions may be asked of the potential juror unless the challenging party has established a prima facie case of bias.

   The challenge is made by saying *"challenge"* before the juror's oath is taken. If the reason for the challenge is simple it will be stated as the challenge is made (e.g. the juror knows D). If the reason is more complex, the other jurors may be asked to leave court so that the challenge can be explained and questions put to the potential juror if the judge so directs.

   If a challenge is successful the potential juror will be replaced by another.

A jury will begin with 12 members. **Up to 3 members of the jury can be discharged** for illness or necessity. The trial must be abandoned if more than 3 jurors have to be discharged.

The **entire jury may be discharged** if:
- It hears inadmissible and prejudicial evidence. Discharge is **not automatic** and will be decided by the judge. The test for discharging the jury is whether there is a **real possibility of injustice** because the evidence has biased the jury;
- It cannot reach a verdict;
- An individual juror has been discharged and there is a risk that he has contaminated the rest of the jury.

If there are multiple Ds and one changes his plea to guilty then the trial should continue against the other Ds, unless being tried by the same jury will cause them particular unfairness.

9.5 The procedural steps in a jury trial

1. **Reading the indictment.**
   Once the jury has been empanelled, the court clerk will read the indictment and state that D has pleaded not guilty.

2. **P opening speech.**
   As in the Magistrates' Court, although it is likely to be a lot longer and will focus the jury's mind on the issues they will need to address (see 9.7 below).

3. **P evidence.**
   As in the Magistrates' Court, the P case can consist of e.g.:
   - Live witnesses (= examination in chief by P; cross-examination by D; any re-examination by P);

   - Read witness statements, **s.9 CJA 1967** (often called *"Section 9 statements"*). P will read the whole document, including the statement of truth. Read witness statements have the **same value as live evidence**. A witness statement may be read where:
     - The evidence is not disputed and the defence has consented;
     - A successful hearsay application has been made.

   - Formal admissions, made under **s.10 CJA 1967** which admit any fact not in dispute (often called *"Section 10 admissions"*).

57

P must call (or offer to call) the witnesses named in the committal/sending bundle unless:

- D agrees to the **witness statement being read; or**
- The witness is **no longer credible** in P's view; **or**
- It makes more sense for **D to call the witness** because his evidence is so contradictory to the P case. In that case, P will tender the witness to the D.

A witness not included in the committal/sending bundle can only be called to give evidence at trial if his witness statement is disclosed to D in a Notice of Further Evidence (NFE). This complies with P's ongoing disclosure duties (see 5.3).

4. **Submission of no case to answer by D.**
   If D chooses to make a submission of no case to answer, it will be made at the end of the P case and before the D case has started. D makes the submission and P has a right of reply. The submission is made in accordance with ***R v Galbraith***[54] and will be successful if:

   - There is **no evidence** that D committed the alleged offence; **or**
   - The evidence **taken at its highest is such that no reasonable jury properly directed could properly convict** [*learn this phrasing word for word!*].

   The submission will fail if:

   - There is evidence on which the jury could properly convict; **and/or**
   - The strength of the case relies on matters exclusively for the jury to decide (e.g. the reliability of a witness).

5. **Defence Case.**
   D is under **no obligation** to call evidence in his own defence, but risks an **adverse inference** if he does not (see 17.5). The D case will proceed in a similar fashion to the P case.

   D may make an opening speech at this point **if he is calling witnesses of fact other than D himself** (i.e. no right to an opening speech if only calling D and/or character witnesses). However, it is rare for D to make an opening speech.

   If testifying, D must do so **before any other live witnesses** unless the judge gives leave to the contrary. If there are multiple Ds the cases will be presented in the order the Ds appear on the indictment. Each D will be cross-examined by his co-Ds first (in the order they appear on the indictment), and by P last.

---

[54] (1981) 73 Cr App R 124.

If D seeks to adduce **alibi** evidence he must **provide particulars of the witness to P in advance**, or risk an **adverse inference.** D may not call expert evidence without the judge's permission if D did not disclose the expert's report to P before the trial.

If D represents himself in person during trial the judge should:
- Ask questions to test the P witnesses;
- Prevent repetitious questioning of P witnesses by D;
- Instruct the jury that D is entitled to represent himself and has been warned about the difficulties of so doing.

6.   **Closing speeches.**
As in the Magistrates' Court, P will give a closing speech first, and D last. Co-Ds make speeches in the order they appear on the indictment (see 9.7).

7.   **Summing up.**
The judge summarises the evidence and explains the law to the jury (see 9.8).

8.   **Jury retires.**
The jury retires to consider their verdict (see 9.9).

9.   **Verdict.**
The jury returns when ready with a verdict. If it cannot reach a verdict it will be discharged and a retrial may be ordered (see 9.9).

10.   **Sentence.**
If D is convicted and an adjournment is not necessary (see 8.3 and section 5 generally).

9.6 Dealing with points of law during the trial

In general, submissions regarding points of law will be **made to the judge in the absence of the jury**. This is because the judge is the tribunal of law, and the jury the tribunal of fact. The judge will make a ruling and then the jury will return to court.

Submissions regarding the admissibility of evidence may be dealt with at the PCMH or during trial. If the submission is made during the trial it should be **made at the point the disputed evidence is about to be called**. The jury will be asked to retire while a point of law is considered.

The court may hold a *voir dire* (= a **trial within a trial**) in which both P and D can call and cross-examine witnesses, to help the judge determine whether the evidence in question is admissible.

9.7 Speeches

Opening speeches

The P opening speech is addressed to the jury. It will normally:
- Give an overview of the P case;
- Outline the witnesses to be called;
- Explain the charges D faces;
- Outline the issues in the case;
- Not refer to any evidence which is to be subject to an admissibility challenge;
- Explain the burden and standard of proof, if wished.

As detailed above, D will not normally make an opening speech, and in any case may only do so if calling witnesses of fact other than just D himself. If D chooses to make an opening speech, it will be after the P case, at the start of the D case.

Closing speeches

P will make its closing speech first. However, as in a summary trial, P **must not** make a closing speech if:
- D is not legally represented; **and**
- D has not called witnesses of fact other than himself.

D makes its closing speech after P. If there are multiple Ds, the speeches will be in the order that the Ds are listed on the indictment.

9.8 The content of summing up

The judge **must** always sum up. In complicated cases, the judge may circulate a draft summing up among counsel and invite them to comment. A deficiency in the summing up can form grounds for an appeal: D has a duty to inform the judge of any deficiency in summing up, and cannot merely leave it to be raised on appeal.

The summing up should contain the elements listed below:

1. **Function of the judge and jury**.
    The law is a matter for the judge and the facts are a matter for the jury. The judge may express views on the facts, but the jury is free to disregard those views.

2. **Burden and standard of proof**.
    It is for the prosecution to prove D's guilt, not for D to prove his innocence. The jury must be satisfied **so that they are sure** that D is guilty.

3.   **Law and evidence.**
       The judge must explain the law and how it relates to the case in a manner that is
       even-handed to both sides. If complicated, written directions on the law may be
       provided to the jury.

4.   **The main features of the evidence** and how it fits into the legal framework.

5.   **Character / Previous convictions.**
       The jury may take into account previous convictions and other evidence of bad
       character that have been adduced at trial, but **bad character does not equate to
       proof of guilt** and the judge must remind the jury of this. It is for the jury to
       decide if the evidence of bad character goes to:
       - **Propensity**: does D (or the complainant or relevant witness) have a
         tendency to commit crimes of this type?
       - **Credibility**: does the bad character of D (or the complainant or relevant
         witness) make him less believable?

       If D has no previous convictions the judge should give a good character (**Vye**)
       direction (see 15.8), stating that it goes both to propensity and credibility.

6.   **Reaching a verdict.**
       Initially the jury should be told that only a unanimous verdict is acceptable; that
       there should be no deliberation unless all members of the jury are present; and
       that each juror has a duty to alert the judge if there are any problems with any of
       the other jurors.

7.   **Directions as required:**
       - A **Turnbull direction** should be given if **identification evidence** is in
         issue (see 18.3);

       - If **expert evidence** has been given the jury should be directed that it is
         not bound by the opinion of the expert;

       - If **lies told by D** are in issue a **Lucas direction** should be given (see
         17.1);

       - If **D has failed to answer police questions**, or **failed to testify in court**
         the jury should be informed:
         - Of the circumstances in which it can draw an adverse
           inference (see chapter 17);
         - That the burden of proof remains on P and any inference
           drawn cannot prove guilt on its own.

       - If D has adduced **alibi evidence** the jury should be directed that:

- Even if it believes the alibi to be false this does not mean D is guilty of the offence;
- The burden of proof remains on P;
- Alibis are sometimes invented to bolster a genuine defence.

- If D has failed to comply with the **requirements of the CPIA 1996** (e.g. by running a defence at trial that is inconsistent with that given in the defence statement, or by not providing the names of witnesses) the jury should be directed that an **adverse inference** may be drawn (see 5.8).

- **Multiple counts or multiple Ds:** the judge must explain that:
  - Each count and each D must be considered separately;
  - Evidence must be disregarded if it is not admissible against a particular D;
  - A decision should be reached based on all of the evidence;
  - A D may run a cut-throat defence (= accusing his co-D) through self-interest;
  - The evidence of a co-D must be treated in the same manner as any other witness.

It is generally **inappropriate** for the judge to comment on the fact that D has not called a particular witness. The judge also has no duty to warn on the dangers of convicting D based on the evidence of an accomplice.

9.9 Verdicts

At the conclusion of the summing up, the jury bailiff will be given charge of the jury. The bailiff takes an oath to:
- Take the jurors to a private place; and
- Not let anyone speak to the jury.

Once the jury has retired it may only communicate with the judge by note. If the note is to do with the trial it should be **read in open court to counsel** in the absence of the jury. Still in the absence of the jury, the judge should **seek counsel's submissions** on the matter contained within the note. After the submissions the judge should give an answer to the jury in open court.

Majority verdicts

The judge can accept a majority verdict after the jury has been deliberating for 2 hours. However the judge should give the jury **at least 2 hours and 10 minutes** to reach a unanimous verdict (to allow for time settling in, etc). This is the minimum time: in longer or more complicated cases, a judge may leave the jury much longer to reach a unanimous verdict.

If the jury returns before 2 hours and 10 minutes (or any longer reasonable time in the circumstances) has passed stating that it is unable to reach a unanimous verdict **it should be sent out again to see if it can.**

When the jury has had enough time and still cannot reach a unanimous verdict it should be told to keep trying, but that **a majority verdict** will now be acceptable. The following verdicts are permissible:
- Jury consists of 12 members: 11-1 or 10-2;
- Jury consists of 11 members: 10-1;
- Jury consists of 10 members: 9-1;
- Jury consists of 9 members: the verdict **must** be unanimous.

No pressure should be put on a jury to reach a verdict. The judge may ask if there is a **reasonable prospect of reaching a verdict**; if none, the judge may discharge the jury.
If the jury is having difficulty reaching a decision the judge may give a:
- Majority verdict direction; **and/or**
- A **Watson**[55] direction to the effect that *"give and take"* is within the scope of the oath taken by the jurors.

If the jury has to separate before it has reached its verdict (e.g. to go home for the night) the judge should direct it that:
- The jury must make its decision based on the evidence and arguments presented in court and **not anything from outside;**
- The evidence has been completed and it would be wrong for the jury to seek further information or evidence;
- Members of the jury must **only discuss the case with each other** and **only in the jury room;**
- Upon leaving court, each juror should try to set the case aside until returning to the jury room.

Lesser offence

The jury can acquit D of a count on the indictment, but convict him of a lesser alternative offence provided that:
- The indictment **expressly or impliedly includes** that lesser offence; and
- The lesser offence can be tried on indictment or is a specified summary offence.[56]

---
[55] [1989] 2 All ER 865.
[56] s.40 CJA 1988.

For example:
- Express: **if words were deleted** from the description of the main offence on the indictment the result would be **the description of the lesser offence** (e.g. *"causing grievous bodily harm with intent"* >> *"causing grievous bodily harm"*);
- Implied: where the **lesser offence is a necessary step** towards the commission of the main offence (e.g. *"dangerous driving"* >> *"careless driving"*).

The jury should consider the lesser charge only once they have considered and acquitted D of the more serious charge. The judge does not have to put the alternative offences before the jury and in deciding whether to do so he must consider:
- Whether there is **a sensible basis on which the jury may convict D for the more serious offence;**
- If the alternative offence will **confuse** the jury or complicate its considerations;
- If the **alleged criminality of D is greater than the alternative**, lesser charge, so that the lesser charge does not properly reflect the P case against D (e.g. an alternative of theft to a charge of robbery would not be appropriate where the main criminality lay in the violence used).

See also 7.4 for pleas to alternative counts.

9.10 Costs after the trial (outline only)

The court may make an order for D's costs to be paid out of central funds (a "defendant's costs order") if:
- D has not been tried for an offence for which he was indicted (i.e. the case against him was dropped); or
- D has been acquitted of any count on the indictment; or
- D is a successful appellant in an appeal from the Magistrates' Court.

Under LASPO 2012, defendant's costs orders are limited to legal aid rates. Moreover, those who seek private representation in the Crown Court will not be entitled to a defendant's costs order at all.

The court can order that only part of D's costs are paid, when he has been acquitted on some counts but convicted on others.

P costs can be awarded if the court is satisfied that D has the means to pay. The order is not intended to be in the nature of a penalty.

The court can order costs against any party which have occurred as a result of an **unnecessary or improper act or omission** by that party. The court also has the power to order a legal or other representative of the party to meet the whole or part of the wasted costs.

10. Preliminary Evidential Matters

10.1 The basic terminology of evidence

Evidence	=	Anything that may prove a fact (e.g. witness testimony, CCTV, bloodstains, etc).
Fact	=	Anything that is accepted to have occurred.
Proof	=	The process or means of convincing an individual that a particular conclusion is correct.
The standard of proof	=	The threshold standard required before a conclusion is deemed to be proven (i.e. *"so that you are sure"* or *"balance of probabilities"*).
Arguments	=	Propositions advanced by advocates (distinct from facts).

10.2 Facts in issue

The facts in issue are **anything that needs to be proved for the case to succeed**, e.g.:
- The identity of the person who committed the offence;
- Whether D's behaviour mounted to the actus reus of the offence;
- Whether D acted with the requisite mens rea;
- Whether D was acting in self-defence or under duress, etc.

The facts in issue are important because they will limit the evidence that can and should be admitted, and can determine who bears the burden of proof on a particular aspect of the case.

A **collateral issue** is an issue taken upon a matter which is not one of the general facts in issue in the case, but which might influence the tribunal of fact (e.g. the credibility of a witness).

10.3 Relevance

Evidence must be relevant to be admissible, and this is a matter of common sense. Evidence is relevant if it **will increase or decrease the probability of a fact in issue being proved**. The evidence need not be directly relevant to a fact in issue (e.g. it could be relevant to a collateral issue such as credibility, or motive), but it must be capable of leading to a particular conclusion.

10.4 Admissibility

The starting point is that evidence is admissible provided that:
- It is **relevant; and**
- It is **not excluded** by a special rule.

Where evidence is excluded by a special rule, it tends to be either because:
- Of the type of evidence it is (e.g. irrelevant previous convictions); or
- It was obtained by unconscionable means (e.g. through torture).

Note that the **court has no power to include inadmissible evidence**; only to exclude otherwise admissible evidence.

There are two main ways by which evidence can be excluded:

1. Common law discretion

Under the common law (**_R v Sang_**[57]), evidence can be excluded if:

Its prejudicial effect outweighs its probative value

Prejudicial effect = The likelihood that the evidence will be used *"the wrong way"* by the jury, e.g. by leading the tribunal of fact to false conclusions, or by tempting the tribunal of fact to convict D on an inadequate basis.

Probative value = The usefulness of the evidence, to a rational and fair tribunal of fact, in proving a matter.

2. Statutory powers

There are a number of statutory provisions governing the admissibility of evidence, e.g.:
- Bad character (s.100 CJA 2003);
- Hearsay (s.114 CJA 2003);
- Confessions (ss.76 and 76A PACE 1984);
- Unfair evidence (s.78 PACE 1984 – see 16.5 below).

---

[57] [1980] AC 402.

Where possible, evidence is excluded under a statutory power rather than pursuant to the common law discretion.

10.5 Weight

Weight is the extent to which the evidence does prove or disprove a conclusion. It is for the tribunal of fact to decide, and is **subjective** (e.g. the jury decides how much weight to give to the evidence of a key witness, or how much weight to place on D's history of dishonesty, etc).

10.6 Tribunals of fact and law

Generally the **tribunal of fact decides the facts of the case** and the **tribunal of law decides the law** to be applied.

In a Crown Court trial, the **tribunal of fact is the jury**. The tribunal of law is the judge.

In a Magistrates' Court trial, **the tribunals of fact and law are the same.** This can cause potential difficulties, because the same person will decide the admissibility of evidence and the factual issues (and will have to put out of his mind any inadmissible evidence he has just heard when deciding the facts).

It should be noted that the tribunal of law will decide factual matters in the following circumstances:
- During a *voir dire* (see 9.6);
- Deciding the sufficiency of the evidence (i.e. after an application to dismiss a charge or after a submission of no case to answer);
- Deciding the meanings of certain words if given an unusual meaning by statute;
- Determining questions of foreign law;
- Deciding the materiality of a false statement in a perjury trial.

In summing up to the jury, the judge can consider and comment on the evidence; however he is not actually deciding facts.

10.7 Presumptions (outline only)

1. *Presumptions without proof of basic facts.*
   This type of presumption is a way of stating where the burden of proof lies in particular circumstances. The most common is the **presumption of innocence**.

2. *Presumptions with proof of basic facts.*
    This type of presumption allows the court to conclude the existence of a fact based on the proof of a preliminary fact. There are 3 types of presumption under this category:

    - *Irrebuttable presumptions of law (e.g. that no child under 10 can be guilty of an offence);*
    - *Rebuttable presumptions of law (e.g. that a person in captivity is not consenting to sexual intercourse);*
    - *Presumptions of fact (e.g. presumption of continuance of life).*

11. Burden and Standard of Proof

11.1 The distinction between the legal burden and evidential burden of proof

Legal burden of proof   =   **The obligation on a party to prove a fact in issue.** Whether the burden has been discharged (= met) is a matter for the **tribunal of fact.**

Evidential burden of proof   =   **The obligation on a party to adduce enough evidence to make an issue live at trial.** Where D bears the evidential burden, this means enough evidence to leave the jury/Magistrates in reasonable doubt. Whether the burden has been discharged is a matter for the **tribunal of law.**

11.2 The general rule concerning the incidence of the burden of proof, and its exceptions

Legal burden of proof

The general rule is that **P bears the legal burden** to prove all elements of the offence for which D is tried. In most cases, D does not have to prove anything.

There are exceptions to the general rule, where D bears the legal burden (the **reverse burden**):
- The defence of **insanity**;
- **Express** statutory exceptions (e.g. possession of an offensive weapon, where D has to show *"good reason or lawful authority"* for its possession);
- **Implied** statutory exceptions (where D alleges that he benefits from some exemption or excuse not explicitly set out in statute, e.g. when charged with driving otherwise than in accordance with a licence).[58]

In considering the relation between the reverse burden of proof and the ECHR the following should be noted:
- The presumption of innocence is not an absolute right, but the state must justify any derogation from it;
- There must be a compelling reason why the reverse burden is fair and reasonable;

---

[58] s.101 MCA 1980.

- If the reverse burden infringes on the right to a fair trial, the court should read down the provision so that it only places an evidential burden on D. A declaration of incompatibility should only be made as a last resort if reading down is not possible.

Evidential burden of proof

The general rule is that the **party which bears the legal burden of proof also bears the evidential burden.**

However, there are some situations in which D bears the **only the evidential burden** of proof; once this has been discharged **it is for P to disprove the defence.**

Some examples of an evidential burden on D (but a legal burden on P) are:

- Self-defence;
- Duress;
- Non-insane automatism;
- Intoxication;

} Common Law

- Use of reasonable force in preventing a crime;
- The defence of loss of control when charged with murder;
- Consent to sexual intercourse, when there exists a rebuttable presumption of no consent;
- Reasonable excuse to be in possession of certain materials.

} Statutory

11.3 The standard of proof when the legal burden rests on the prosecution

The standard of proof when the legal burden rests on P is that the tribunal of fact **must be sure that D is guilty.** This form of words was devised to avoid the problems juries encountered with the traditional direction of *"beyond reasonable doubt"*. However, both phrases mean the same thing.

11.4 The standard of proof when the legal burden rests on the defence

The standard of proof when the legal burden rests on D is **the balance of probabilities** (*"more likely than not"*). D **never** has to prove anything beyond reasonable doubt.

12. Preliminary Issues Relating to Witnesses

12.1 Competence and compellability

The starting assumption is that:
- All persons are competent; **and**
- All competent persons are compellable.

Competent   =   A person **can legally be called** to give evidence. The court must be satisfied that the witness is competent on the balance of probabilities. **Nobody is incompetent on the basis of age alone**, but a witness will not be competent where he:
- Cannot understand questions put to him; **or**
- Cannot give comprehensible answers.

Compellable   =   A person can be **forced** by the court to give evidence. Examples of witnesses that are competent but **not** compellable are:
- Heads of State;
- Judges;
- Bankers (only compellable on a judge's order);
- **D** (see below);
- **D's spouse** (see below).

Compellability of D

D is not competent to give evidence for P (i.e. against his co-Ds) until/unless:
- He pleads **guilty**;
- He is **acquitted**;
- **Separate trials** have been ordered;
- Following an order of ***nolle prosequi*** (= do not prosecute) by the Attorney General.

In any of these scenarios, D becomes both competent and compellable.

D is competent to give evidence on his own behalf or for a co-D, but cannot be compelled to do so (remember, D normally does not have to prove anything, and can remain silent at trial).

Compellability of D's spouse

The spouse or civil partner of D is **competent to give evidence for any party**, and is **compellable to give evidence for D**. However the spouse is not **compellable for P**, except where D has been charged with:

- Assaulting or injuring the spouse, or threatening to do so;
- Assaulting or injuring a person under the age of 16, or threatening to do so;
- A sexual offence against a person under the age of 16;
- Aiding, abetting, counselling, procuring or inciting any of the above.

These rules do not apply to those who merely co-habit, or to former spouses. These rules also only apply where the spouse is not him/herself a co-D.

12.2 Oaths and affirmations

Witnesses give **sworn evidence**, which means the evidence is given under oath.
The oath is valid if:
- It appears to the court to be binding on the conscience of the witness; **and**
- The witness considers it binding on his conscience.

Different oaths are available for different religions, or the witness can choose to make a *"solemn affirmation"* (which is not sworn on a holy book and makes no reference to God) if he objects to the oath. The oath is binding even if the witness holds no religious belief.

A witness may not give sworn evidence unless:
- He has attained the **age of 14**; and
- He has **sufficient understanding** of the solemnity of the occasion and the responsibility created by the oath to tell the truth.

If a witness is not permitted to give sworn evidence, then the evidence must be unsworn. The weight of this evidence is a matter for the tribunal of fact.

If the witness is **under 17**, he may make a **promise** instead of an oath/affirmation.

12.3 The principles and procedure for the issue of a witness summons and warrant of arrest (outline only)

A witness summons will be granted if:
- The witness is likely to give material evidence; and
- The witness will not attend voluntarily; and
- It is in the interests of justice to do so.

If the witness does not respond to the summons a **warrant can be issued for his arrest.** Failure to attend to give evidence after the issue of a summons can be punished as contempt of court.

The party requiring a witness summons must apply to the court. The application may be made orally and must:

- *Identify the proposed witness;*
- *Explain what evidence the witness can give;*
- *Explain why the evidence is likely to be material;*
- *Explain why it is in the interests of justice to issue the summons.*

13. The Examination of Witnesses

P should call (or offer to call) **everyone who gives evidence of the primary facts of the case, even if inconsistent**, unless they are unworthy of belief. Both P and D can call witnesses in any order, although:

- If giving evidence, D should testify before any other D witnesses.[59] The court has a discretion to vary this;
- Expert witnesses can be called at any time (even before D himself).

Neither side can call evidence after the close of its case, except:

- Matters arising that could not have been foreseen (e.g. evidence in rebuttal);
- Evidence accidentally omitted.

The judge has a wide discretion to allow any evidence to be called after the close of the case, but should only exercise it rarely.

Neither side can **ever** call evidence after verdict.

Both the Magistrates and the judge can call and examine any witnesses.

13.1 Examination in chief

Questioning

Questions asked during examination in chief should be **non-leading**. Such questions do not suggest the answer sought, and do not assume the existence of a fact which has not been established. They tend to begin with words such as who, what, when, where, why, etc.

Non-leading questions **do not** need to be used for:

- Introductory matters such as the name of the witness;
- Matters not in dispute;
- Hostile witnesses (see below).

Memory refreshing

Before giving evidence, a witness may refresh his memory from (i.e. re-read) his witness statement outside court. He does not need the permission of the court to do this.

---

[59] s.79 PACE 1984.

Whilst giving evidence, a witness may refresh his memory from a document at any stage provided that he:[60]

1. Uses a document made or verified by him (e.g. a witness statement) and states in oral evidence that the document sets out his recollection of events:
   "Did you make a witness statement about these events?"

2. States that the document was made closer to the time of the event in question:
   "When did you make that statement?"

3. States that his recollection at the time the document was made was better than it is now:
   "Was your memory of the events better at the time of making the statement than it is now?"

Any document used to refresh a witness's memory must be available for inspection by the other parties, who may cross-examine the witness on the memory refreshing document. However, if the cross-examination goes beyond the actual portion of the document used to refresh the witness's memory, the whole document may be put in as evidence by the party calling the witness.[61]

The memory refreshing document may be put before the jury if it:
- Will assist in determining an issue; **and/or**
- Will be hard for the jury to follow the cross-examination otherwise; **and/or**
- Is a convenient aide-memoire to lengthy evidence given by the witness.

Previous consistent statements

In general it is **not permissible** to adduce evidence of a witness's previous consistent statements. This is to prevent a potentially false account being seen as credible merely because the witness has repeated it. Most previous statements will also be **hearsay** evidence in any case (see chapter 14).

This general rule is subject to the following **six** exceptions:[62]

1. **Memory refreshing** documents (e.g. his witness statement) – see above.

2. **Previous identification** of a person, object or place.

3. Statements adduced in **rebuttal** of a suggestion of recent fabrication.

---

[60] s.139(1) CJA 2003.
[61] s.120(3) CJA 2003.
[62] s.120 CJA 2003.

4.   Previous **complaints** in these specified circumstances:
- The witness is the person the offence was committed against; **and**
- The proceedings relate to that offence; **and**
- The statement of the witness consists of a complaint, which if true proves the offence or part of the offence; **and**
- The complaint was not a result of a threat; **and**
- The witness gives oral evidence on the matter before the statement is adduced. It does not matter if the complaint was elicited by a leading question.

5.   An exculpatory (= denying) statement made **on accusation**. This is admissible as evidence of consistency and therefore creditworthiness. A statement which is a mixture of admissions and exculpatory statements (**mixed statements** – e.g. *"It was me who punched him but it was only in self-defence"*) should be admitted complete in order for the tribunal of fact to determine where the truth lies.

6.   **Res gestae** (= any act or statement so closely associated in time, place or circumstance with a matter in issue that it can be regarded as part of the same transaction).

Hostile witnesses

Generally it is not permitted for a party to impeach the credibility of its own witness by using leading questions, previous inconsistent statements or bad character evidence (although bad character may be introduced if it is relevant and the purpose is not to impeach the credibility of the witness). This is so even if the witness does not come up to proof or gives unfavourable evidence (an *"unfavourable witness"*).

However, where the witness is more than merely unfavourable and is **not desirous of telling the truth to the court**, the calling party may apply to treat the witness as **hostile**.[63] If the application is granted, the party calling that witness may:
- Ask leading questions; **and**
- Put to the witness any previous inconsistent statements; **and**
- Contradict the witness using other evidence.

In essence, this amounts to cross-examining one's own witness. Note that **bad character evidence cannot be called** against a hostile witness.

If the hostile witness confirms a previous inconsistent statement, it will stand as his evidence. However, if he does not then his oral testimony and the previous statement will both be entered in evidence, and it will be for the tribunal of fact to decide which it prefers.

---

[63] s.3 Criminal Procedure Act 1865.

The purpose of cross-examination is to:
- Elicit favourable evidence from a witness;
- Put your case to a witness;
- Qualify, weaken and cast doubt on the case of the other party.

In general the questions asked during cross-examination should be **leading**. Such questions suggest the answer sought (e.g. *"X is true, isn't it?"*).

A witness is liable to cross-examination unless he:
- Produced documents without being sworn;
- Was called by mistake;
- Was called by the judge.

The principal consequence of not cross-examining is that in closing, a party cannot invite the tribunal of fact to believe a point that has not been put to D or the witness.

If a witness dies before cross-examination, his examination in chief will remain valid evidence.

Restrictions on cross-examination when conducted by D in person

Where D represents himself, he cannot cross-examine:
- **The complainant, when D is charged with a sexual offence.** This restriction only extends to cross-examination about that offence or any connected offence. In practice, counsel will be appointed by the court (under a **section 38 order**) to cross-examine on all matters on D's behalf.[64]

- A **child witness** about the main offence or any related offence, **if** the main offence is:
    - A sexual offence;
    - Kidnap, child abduction or false imprisonment;
    - An offence involving assault, injury or the threat of injury;
    - Child cruelty.

The court also has a **statutory discretion to stop D cross-examining in person <u>any</u> witness**. It can exercise this discretion of its own motion, or on the application of P. However, if it does exercise its discretion, the court must invite D to obtain legal representation. The court may appoint a legal representative for D if it is in the interests of justice (under a section 38 order: see above).

---

[64] ss.34-38 YJCEA 1999.

77

The judge also has a common law power to restrict the length and topics of cross-examination.

Restrictions on cross-examination by counsel

The judge has a common law discretion to stop counsel from conducting improper and/or unnecessary cross-examination, and to restrict the length and topics of cross-examination. The Code of Conduct also places limits on cross-examinations conducted by counsel.

Cross-examination cannot be used to elicit inadmissible evidence.

Previous inconsistent statements

A witness **can** be cross-examined on any previous **inconsistent** statements made by him (in contrast to the rule relating to previous consistent statements).

If the witness **denies** the previous inconsistent statement, that previous statement is admissible as to his **credibility, but not proof of its contents.**

If the witness **accepts and adopts** the previous inconsistent statement, it is admissible **BOTH as to credibility AND as proof of its contents.**

Witness credibility

Questions in cross-examination which impugn (= attack) the character of a witness are proper if they will seriously affect the opinion of the court as to the witness's credibility.

Questioning will be improper if:
- It will not or will only very slightly affect the opinion of the court; **and/or**
- There is great disproportion between the impugning of the witness's character and the importance of the witness's evidence.

Finality on collateral matters

The answer given by a witness to a collateral issue is final and it is not permitted to adduce further evidence to prove matters to the contrary, **unless** it involves:
- A previous conviction;[65]
- A suggestion of bias;
- A reputation for untruthfulness;
- A disability affecting reliability.

---

[65] s.6 Criminal Procedure Act 1865.

This is to prevent the trial process being side-tracked into discussing infinite collateral issues.

Complainants of sexual offences

There is a general restriction on cross-examining the complainant of a sexual offence about his/her sexual behaviour. This is to prevent D impugning the character of the P witness based on his/her sexual history when such history has insufficient relevance to the case, and/or is likely to prejudice the jury unfairly against the P witness.

Questions or evidence of sexual behaviour will **only** be allowed if:[66]
- A refusal to do so would render any conviction unsafe; **and**
- Any of the following applies:
  - It relates to an issue **other than consent**;
  - It relates to consent and behaviour **on or about the same time as the alleged offence**;
  - It relates to consent and the previous **behaviour cannot be explained as a coincidence** because:
    - It is so similar to the alleged offence; or
    - It is so similar to other sexual behaviour at or at about the same time as the alleged offence;
  - It is adduced to **rebut or explain evidence** adduced by P about the complainant's previous sexual behaviour, and would go no further than necessary.

A party wishing to cross-examine on the previous sexual behaviour of the complainant **must make a written application** to do so, no later than 28 days after prosecution disclosure.

13.3 Re-examination

The rules for re-examining the witness are the **same as for examination in chief**. The subjects covered in re-examination must be limited to topics covered in cross-examination.

13.4 Special measures

A witness will be eligible for special measures if any of the following applies:[67]
- He is **under the age of 18**;

---

[66] s.41 YJCEA 1999.
[67] ss.16-17 YJCEA 1999.

- The quality of his evidence will be diminished, because he:
    o Suffers from a **mental disorder**; or
    o Has an **impairment of intelligence** or social functioning; or
    o Has a **physical disability** or disorder.

- The quality of his evidence will be diminished by **fear or distress** at giving evidence. In deciding, the court should consider:
    o The offence;
    o The age of the witness;
    o The social, cultural and ethnic background of the witness;
    o The politics and religion of the witness;
    o The behaviour of D and his associates towards the witness.

- He is the **complainant in a sexual offence** case.

If the witness is eligible for special measures, the court will consider which particular special measure would be appropriate and would maximise the quality as far as practicable.

The following special measures are available:
- Using a screen to block the witness from D's view;
- Giving evidence via *"live link"* (= video link from another room);
- Removal of wigs and gowns;
- Pre-recording the examination in chief;
- Pre-recording the cross-examination and re-examination;
- Using an intermediary (not available for a witness in fear);
- Using a device so that the witness can communicate with another person during the examination (not available for a witness in fear);
- Excluding specified persons from court (only for those in fear, or the complainant in a sex case).

Witnesses under 18 will, **by default**, give evidence via a pre-recorded video and live link, unless it is not in the interests of justice and will not maximise their evidence.

Application for special measures should be made in writing **within 14 days** of a not guilty indication (in the Magistrates' Court), or **within 28 days** of service of documents (in the Crown Court).

Witness anonymity order

The court has the power to grant a **witness anonymity order**. This means that:
- The witness's name will not be released to the public or the other parties;
- The witness will be screened from the court;
- Voice modulation technology will be used when he gives evidence;
- No questions may be asked which might identify him directly or indirectly.

Such an order is an extreme measure and will **only** be made if **all** the following conditions are met:

- It is necessary to protect the safety of the witness or prevent real harm to the public interest; **and**
- It is consistent with a fair trial; **and**
- The importance of the testimony of the witness is such that in the interests of justice the witness ought to testify; **and**
- Without such an order:
  - The witness will not testify; **or**
  - There will be real harm to the public interest.

Any form of special measure could prevent effective testing of the witness's evidence, and/or prejudice the jury, so the court will carefully weigh up whether it is necessary, considering:[68]

- Any views expressed by the witness; **and**
- Whether the measure or measures might tend to inhibit such evidence being effectively tested by a party to the proceedings.

---

[68] s.19(3) YJCEA 1999.

14. Hearsay Evidence

You should read and familiarise yourself with
ss.114 - 126 CJA 2003

14.1 The definition of hearsay under the Criminal Justice Act 2003

Hearsay is:

> A statement
>
> Not made in oral evidence in proceedings
>
> Whose purpose was to cause another person to believe the matter stated, or to cause a person or machine to act on the basis that it is true.

A statement is **any representation of fact or opinion, made by a person, by whatever means**. This includes a representation made in a sketch, photofit or pictorial form.

14.2 The difference between hearsay and original evidence

Original evidence is a repetition of a third party's statement, but **not** to establish the truth of what was asserted. It is adduced to establish some other fact, e.g.:

- The speaker's state of mind (*"my child is going to die!"* to demonstrate that the speaker was upset, but not to prove that the child was going to die);
- A listener's state of mind (*"this coat is old"* to demonstrate that the listener would have thought coat was old, but not to prove that the coat was actually old);
- To show a statement was made (*"I stole the watch"* to prove that something was said, rather than to prove that the speaker stole the watch).

14.3 The difference between hearsay and real evidence

Real evidence is **physical, tangible evidence**, such as an object, photograph or computer print-out.

A document will be real evidence and not hearsay where it is admitted in evidence **not to prove the truth of its contents**, but rather to prove some other fact (such as its existence or its condition).

A computer print-out, reading or other information will be real evidence and not hearsay if **it has been produced automatically by a device with no manual input** (e.g. the results of a breathalyser are real evidence, as they are generated automatically and no data is entered manually by the operator). The information provided by such a device is not a statement by a person and so is not hearsay.

However, if such evidence relies on the input of a person for its accuracy (e.g. the results of a calculation, where the original figures were entered by a human), it will not be admissible unless it is proved that the underlying information is accurate.

IS A STATEMENT HEARSAY?

1. Is it a representation of fact or opinion?
2. If so, was it made by a person (whether directly or indirectly)?

    no = real evidence

    yes = continue to stage 3

3. Was the purpose of the maker of the statement:
    (a) To cause another to believe the matter stated; or
    (b) To cause another to act (or a machine to operate) on the basis that it is true?

    no = original evidence

    yes = continue to stage 4

4. Is the purpose of adducing the statement to prove the matter stated?

    no = original evidence

    yes = hearsay evidence

14.4 General restriction on the admissibility of hearsay evidence

Generally hearsay evidence is admissible **if, and only if**, it falls within one of the following exceptions from s.114(1) CJA 2003:
- A statutory provision;
- A preserved common law exception;
- All parties agree to its admission;
- It is in the interests of justice to admit it.

The witness is unavailable[69]

The evidence of an unavailable witness (usually, their witness statement) may be admissible if:
- The maker of the statement could have given admissible oral evidence; **and**
- The maker of the statement can be identified; **and**
- The maker of the statement is unavailable due to one of the following:
    - Death;
    - Unfitness to testify due to a physical or mental condition;
    - Being outside the UK and it not being reasonably practicable to secure attendance;
    - Cannot be found despite all reasonably practicable steps being taken;
    - Fear at giving evidence.

Note that it is **not enough that the witness would simply prefer not to give evidence** – their unavailability **must** be due to one of these reasons.

The statement was made in a business or professional document[70]

A business or professional document may be admissible if:
- Oral evidence of the same matter would be admissible; **and**
- The document was:
    - Created or received in the course of a trade, business, profession or other occupation; **and**
    - The supplier of the information must have had (or reasonably have been supposed to have had) personal knowledge of the facts; **and**
    - If the information has passed from person to person, each must have done so in the course of his occupation.

Further, if the document was prepared for a criminal investigation or proceedings (e.g. a witness statement), then **in addition** to the above criteria either:
- The criteria for the witness being unavailable must be fulfilled; **or**
- The maker of the statement cannot reasonably be expected to remember its contents.

---

[69] s.116 CJA 2003.
[70] s.117 CJA 2003.

Previous statements

The **previous inconsistent statements** of a witness who has given oral evidence are admissible as evidence.[71]

Additionally the previous statements of a witness are admissible in any of the following circumstances:[72]

- To rebut the suggestion of fabrication;
- Where the witness cannot be expected to remember;
- Where the witness has made a previous complaint;
- Where the witness has made a previous identification.

See also 13.1 on previous consistent statements.

Interests of justice[73]

In deciding whether to admit the evidence in the interests of justice the following factors should be considered:

- The probative value of the evidence;
- Other evidence available;
- The importance of the evidence to the case;
- The circumstances in which the statement was made;
- The reliability of the statement maker;
- The reliability of the evidence that the statement was made;
- Whether oral evidence could be given and if not why;
- The difficulty challenging such evidence;
- The prejudice that the evidence may cause.

Care must be taken to ensure that this provision is not be used to circumvent the stricter provisions of the other gateways, but it should not be applied so narrowly as to have no effect.

Preserved common law exceptions

The CJA 2003 preserved the following **eight** exceptions to the hearsay rule:[74]

- Public information (e.g. maps, public records or a date of birth);

- Reputation as to character (i.e. that D is of good or bad character);

---

[71] s.119 CJA 2003.
[72] s.120 CJA 2003.
[73] s.114(1)(d) CJA 2003.
[74] s.118 CJA 2003.

- Reputation or family tradition (to prove/disprove the existence of a marriage; of public or general right; or the identity of a third person or thing);

- **Res gestae**, where any of the below apply:
  - The maker was **so emotionally overpowered** that the possibility of the matter stated being concocted is impossible. The test is:
    1. Can concoction be disregarded? **AND**
    2. Was there an unusual or startling or dramatic event and if so:
       - Did the event dominate the thoughts of the maker? **and**
       - Was the statement an instinctive reaction to the event? **and**
       - Was the statement made approximately contemporaneously?

  - The hearsay statement was **accompanied by an act** which can be evaluated as evidence only if accompanied by the statement;

  - The statement relates to an **intention or emotion**. Note that it cannot prove the cause of that physical state.

- Confessions (only admissible at common law against the maker of the confession himself, but not generally admissible against his co-Ds);

- Confessions by agents;

- Common enterprise: where D1, **during the crime**, says something that implicates D2, that statement is admissible as to the truth of its contents. But the following must be shown:
  - Common criminal enterprise (= wider than conspiracy, and will normally be where Ds are jointly charged); **and**
  - That the statement was made to pursue that end (not merely a consequence of it).

- Expert evidence.

On multiple hearsay[75]

Multiple hearsay = e.g. A repeating what B repeated from C.

---

[75] s.121 CJA 2003.

Multiple hearsay is not admissible unless:
- Either of the hearsay statements is admissible under s.117 (business documents), s.119 (inconsistent statements) or s.120 (other previous statements – see above) of the CJA 2003; **or**
- All parties agree; **or**
- It is necessary in the interests of justice.

14.6 How to make applications to adduce hearsay evidence

A party **must serve notice** on the court officer and every other party if it wishes to introduce hearsay evidence under the provisions for:
- The interests of justice;
- An unavailable witness;
- Multiple hearsay.

If the introducing party fails to do so:
- The evidence will not be admissible without the court's permission;
- If leave is given to admit the evidence, adverse inferences may be drawn;
- There may be cost consequences.

The notice must:
- Identify the hearsay;
- Set out the facts relied upon;
- Explain how the facts will be proved;
- Explain why the evidence is admissible;
- Have attached any unserved document or statement which contains the hearsay.

The notice should be introduced **by P not more than 14 days after D's guilty plea**; or **by D as soon as reasonably practicable**. The court has the power to extend the time limits, even if they have expired.

14.7 Excluding hearsay evidence

Hearsay evidence can be excluded by:
- A general statutory discretion to exclude hearsay evidence **if the dangers of admission substantially outweigh the benefits**;[76]
- s.78 PACE (see 16.5);
- Any other discretionary power of the court to exclude evidence.

---

[76] s.126(1) CJA 2003.

Business documents etc can be excluded if the court decides that they are unreliable owing to the source of the information, or to how the document was supplied or received.

The court can also stop the case if the evidence admitted creates a risk of an unsafe conviction.[77] Further, hearsay evidence **cannot be used to sidestep the rules regarding competence**. The maker of the hearsay statement must have been competent to give evidence at the time of making the statement.[78]

A hearsay statement can be challenged in 3 ways:
- Evidence can be admitted **challenging the credibility** of its maker;[79]
- Proof of **previous inconsistent statements** can be admitted;
- Evidence may with the court's leave be given of any matter which (if he had given such evidence) could have been put to him in cross-examination as relevant to his credibility as a witness but of which evidence could not have been adduced by the cross-examining party.

14.8 Procedural requirements relating to applications to exclude

Any party opposing the admission of hearsay evidence must apply to the court to determine the objection. The application must be served on the court and all other parties.

The application must be served **within 14 days** of the last of:
- Service of the hearsay notice;
- Service of the evidence;
- D pleading not guilty.

The application must explain:
- Which facts in the hearsay notice are disputed;
- Why the evidence is inadmissible;
- Any other objection.

---

[77] s.125 CJA 2003.
[78] s.123 CJA 2003.
[79] s.124 CJA 2003.

15. Character Evidence

15.1 Definition of bad character under the Criminal Justice Act 2003[80]

Bad character = Evidence of **misconduct**, or a **disposition towards misconduct**, defined as:

- The commission of an **offence**. This is interpreted broadly and includes:
  - Previous convictions;
  - Other counts on the indictment;
  - Offences for which D was never prosecuted;
  - Offences for which D was prosecuted and acquitted.

- **Other reprehensible behaviour**. It is for the court to decide whether or not the conduct is reprehensible.

The definition of bad character **does not include** evidence that:
- Has to do with the offence with which D is charged; or
- Is of misconduct connected to the prosecution or investigation of the offence.

15.2 The gateways for the admissibility of non-defendant bad character

The bad character of a non-D is **generally not admissible** unless one of the below applies:[81]

- All parties agree; **or**

- It is **important explanatory evidence**, i.e.:
  - Without it the court or jury would find it impossible or difficult properly to understand other evidence in the case; **and**
  - Its value for understanding the case as a whole is substantial; **or**

- It is of **substantial probative value** in relation to a matter in issue in the proceedings **AND is substantially important to the case as a whole.** Matters in issue include both facts and credibility. In considering probative value, the court must assess:
  - The nature and number of events;

---

[80] s.98 CJA 2003.
[81] s.100 CJA 2003.

- ○ When the events are alleged to have occurred;
- ○ Where relevant, the similarities between each of the alleged instances of misconduct;
- ○ Where relevant, the extent to which the evidence shows the same person was responsible for the misconduct each time.

15.3 The gateways for admissibility of defendant bad character

s.101(1) CJA 2003 provides 7 gateways which can be used to admit D's bad character. Once the evidence has been admitted it can be used for **any purpose to which it is relevant**, irrespective of the gateway used.

The 7 gateways are listed fully below, but here is a quick way to remember them:[82]

> **s.101(1):**
> (a) **Agree**
> (b) **Blabs**
> (c) **Context**
> (d) **Done it before**   [Only P]
> (e) **'e did it!**   [Only D]
> (f) **False impression**   [Only P]
> (g) **Gets at the witness**

s.101(1)(a)   **All parties agree** to the admission of the evidence.

s.101(1)(b)   **D introduces the evidence himself.**

This is rare, but may be done for tactical reasons (see 15.6). D may adduce the evidence as part of his case or give it in response to a question asked in cross-examination designed to elicit it.

s.101(1)(c)   The evidence is **important explanatory evidence** (i.e. provides the context). This gateway can be used by either P or D (against a co-D).

Just as for a non-D, evidence is important explanatory evidence if:
- Without it the court or jury would find it impossible or difficult properly to understand other evidence in the case; and
- Its value for understanding the case as a whole is **substantial**.

---

[82] This was first devised by Jacqui Beeley of Kaplan Law School and is reproduced with her kind permission.

s.101(1)(d) The evidence is relevant to **an important matter in issue between the P and the D.**

It can **only be used by P**. This gateway is often used to show that D has *"done it before"* (similar fact evidence) and therefore is more likely to have done it this time. s.103(1) states that an *"important matter in issue"* includes:

- D's **propensity to commit this type of offence** UNLESS such a propensity makes it no more likely that he is guilty this time (e.g. where he fully admits his actions but argues that in law they don't amount to an offence);
- D's **propensity to be untruthful,** EXCEPT where it is not suggested that D's account is untruthful in the current proceedings.

Propensity to commit this kind of offence

The main test for determining whether propensity evidence is admissible is taken from **_R v Hanson_**:[83]

> 1. Does the conviction history establish propensity?
> 2. Does propensity make it more likely that D is guilty of the current offence?
> 3. Would it be unjust to rely on the previous convictions, and would admitting the previous convictions make the trial unfair?

Also from **_Hanson_**:

- There is no minimum number of events required to establish propensity, but the fewer the events the less likely it is that propensity will be established;
- Generally propensity will be established if there are a large number of previous convictions or the previous conviction(s) have a striking factual similarity to the current offence;
- P must decide, at the time of giving notice, whether to rely only on the fact of D's conviction, or also on its circumstances;
- It is often necessary to examine the detail of each conviction and not just the name of the offence;
- If there is a large gap between the date on which the offence was committed and the date of conviction, the date of commission is more significant.

---

[83] [2005] EWCA Crim 824.

Propensity to be untruthful

Evidence of D's untruthfulness in the past is **generally only relevant if dishonesty is an element** of the offence charged,[84] e.g. fraud, deception, perjury etc.

s.101(1)(e)   The evidence has **substantial probative value** to an **important matter in issue between co-Ds.**

This gateway can **only be used by D against a co-D**. It cannot be used by P. It is used when co-Ds are running cut-throat defences (i.e. each D blames his co-D).

There is **no power to exclude** this evidence under the CJA 2003 or common law because D's defence should not be fettered, even if it comes at the expense of a co-D's defence. However, the evidence can be excluded by the court if there has been a breach of the notice requirements under the CrimPR.

s.101(1)(f)   Evidence to **correct a false impression** given by D.

D will be regarded as having given a false impression if he makes an express or implied assertion that gives the court a false or misleading impression about him (e.g. states that he has never been in trouble before when he has a criminal record).

D is responsible for any assertion:
- He makes in the proceedings, whether or not it is in the evidence he personally gives;
- He makes under caution but before charge, if evidence of that assertion is given in the proceedings;
- He makes on being charged if evidence of that assertion is given in the proceedings;
- Made by a witness called by D;
- Made by any witness cross-examined by D with the intention of eliciting the assertion;
- Made by any person outside of the court, which is adduced by D.

An express or implied assertion even includes D's conduct or dress.

---

[84] *R v Campbell* [2007] EWCA Crim 1472.

To be admissible the bad character evidence must be capable of rebutting the false impression, and it must **go no further than rebutting** the false impression.

s.101(1)(g)   D has **attacked the character of another person**.

Only P can use this gateway. D is deemed to attack another person's character if:
- He adduces evidence attacking that person's character;
- He deliberately elicits such evidence in cross-examination;
- Evidence is given of D attacking the other person's character when questioned under caution before charge;
- Evidence is given of D attacking the other person's character when charged;
- D accuses a co-D of the crime and/or the police of improper conduct.

15.4 How to make applications to adduce bad character evidence[85]

In respect of a **non-D's bad character**, the adducing party must **apply** for permission to adduce evidence of bad-character.

In respect of **D's bad character**, the adducing party must **give notice** of an intention to adduce evidence of D's bad character.

A notice of intent to introduce bad character must be served on every other party and the court. The notice must contain:
- The facts of the misconduct;
- How these facts will be proved if disputed;
- Why the evidence is admissible.

If P intends to adduce the evidence, the notice must be served **within 14 days** of D's not guilty plea. If D intends to introduce the evidence against his co-D, the notice should be served as soon as possible and **not more than 14 days** after P has disclosed the material on which the notice is based. The court has the power to vary the time limits and requirements of the notice.

The court may determine the matter with or without a hearing. However, it must not make a determination unless:
- Each party other than the applicant is present; **or**
- Each party has had at least 14 days to object.

---

[85] See CrimPR Part 35.

The court must give its reasons in public, but without the jury present.

Where the issue arises at trial (for example, D in his examination in chief gives a false impression of his character), the notice requirements do not apply. The adducing party can give oral notice or make an oral application.

15.5 How to make applications to exclude bad character evidence

Evidence which could be admitted under the gateways may be excluded under:
- s.78 PACE 1984;
- s.101(3) CJA 2003 **(only for gateways d and g)**;
- The common law;
- The CrimPR for a breach of the notice requirement.

s.101(3) CJA 2003, which only applies to gateways d and g, states that the court should not admit evidence through this gateway if:
- D makes an application to exclude the evidence; **and**
- It appears that the evidence will have **such an adverse effect on the fairness of the proceedings that it ought not to be admitted.**

Bad character evidence which P wishes to adduce to show propensity under gateway d can also be excluded if it would be **unjust to admit it** due to the passage of time or some other reason.[86]

Any party objecting to the introduction of D's bad character must apply to the court to determine the objection, serving the application **not more than 14 days** after receiving the notice seeking to introduce the evidence.

The application must include **all** of the following:
- The misconduct which is disputed;
- The facts and misconduct admitted;
- Why the evidence is not admissible;
- Why it would be unfair to admit the evidence;
- Any other objections.

The court may determine the matter with or without a hearing. However, it must not make a determination unless the party which served the notice:
- Is present; **or**
- Had a reasonable opportunity to respond.

---

[86] s.103(3) CJA 2003.

The judge has the power to stop a trial if the bad character evidence admitted is so contaminated as to render the conviction unsafe. In such circumstances the judge can direct an acquittal or discharge the jury.

Note that if D is 21 years old or over, evidence of convictions for offences committed when he was under 14 is not admissible unless:[87]
- Both the current and previous offence could be tried by indictment only; **and**
- It is in the interests of justice to admit it.

15.6 Tactical use of character evidence

The most common use of character evidence at trial is by P, against D. However, bad character evidence may be admitted by either side for tactical reasons. For example:

- P may also adduce a non-D's bad character to prove that a person other than D is guilty of an offence, which is an essential requirement for the offence with which D is charged (e.g. in order to prove a charge of handling, the goods involved must have been stolen).

- D may adduce a non-D's or a co-D's bad character evidence tactically, e.g. to:
  - Support the suggestion that the offence was committed by a person other than D;
  - Bolster a defence;
  - Support an allegation of police malpractice.

- D may adduce D's own bad character tactically, e.g. to:
  - Avoid jury speculation about D's failure to assert good character;
  - Allow him to attack another person's character, without D's bad character being exposed in response;
  - Allow D's explanation to be fully understood, where D's actions are only explicable when the context is known.

15.7 Proving convictions under ss.73-75 PACE

Under s.73 PACE 1984 a previous conviction can be proved by a **certificate of conviction** signed by an officer of the convicting court. P must call witnesses to:
- Produce the certificate of conviction; **and**
- Confirm that D (or the witness) is the person named on the certificate.

Under s.74 PACE, the fact that a non-D was convicted of an offence will be taken as evidence that the non-D committed that offence unless proved otherwise.

---

[87] s.16(2) CYPA 1963.

Under s.75 PACE, where evidence that a person has been convicted of an offence is admissible through s.74 PACE, the following can be used to prove the facts on which the conviction was based:

- Any document admitted as evidence of the conviction;
- The contents of the information, complaint, indictment or charge sheet on which the person in question was convicted (or the equivalent documents if the person was charged in another EU member state).

15.8 Good character directions

A good character direction (**Vye direction**) should be given if D is of good character. The terms of the direction were established in **R v Vye**[88] which held that:

- Regarding credibility, a D of good character is **more likely to be telling the truth**;
- Regarding guilt, a D of good character is **less likely to have committed the offence.**

If D has previous convictions but they are not relevant or were acquired a long time ago, he may be considered as of **effective good character**, and the judge can decide whether to give a good character direction, in whole or in part.

If there are multiple Ds, but not all have good character, the judge will give a good character direction for those Ds entitled to one. It is within the judge's discretion whether to state that evidence of good character has not been provided by the other Ds, or not mention the matter.

---

[88] [1993] 1 WLR 471.

16. Confessions and Unlawfully Obtained Evidence

Read and familiarise yourself with ss.76 and 76A PACE 1984

16.1 The definition of confessions under PACE

A confession is defined by s.82(1) PACE as any statement **wholly or partly adverse to the person who made it**, whether made to a person in authority or not, and whether made in words or otherwise. This is a wide definition.

16.2 The principles governing the admissibility of confessions

PACE governs the admissibility of confessions. If a confession is admissible, **the whole statement which contains the confession is admissible**, even if it is partly exculpatory.

s.76 PACE: confessions adduced by P

A confession made by D is admissible against him provided it is:
- Relevant to a matter in issue; **and**
- Not excluded by the court.

Confessions are only **evidence of facts actually known** by the maker of the statement.

In a case with multiple Ds, if D1 makes a confession which incriminates D2, the confession is **only evidence against D1**. However, the jury can consider D1 and his confession first and then use a finding of guilt against D1 as a fact to be used evidentially against D2. Before they can do this, the jury must be sure that the confession of D1 is the truth.

If D1 confesses in the presence of D2, who acknowledges the incriminating comments so as to adopt them, then the confession becomes admissible against both Ds.

The court has the discretion to edit a confession.

s.76A PACE: confessions adduced by a co-D

A confession made by a D in the same proceedings can be adduced against him by a co-D provided it is:
- Relevant to a matter in issue; **and**
- Not excluded by the court.

s.76A PACE does not apply when his co-D has pleaded guilty. This is because a person who has pleaded guilty and is not on trial is no longer a person charged with an offence, and so no longer a co-D.

16.3 The admissibility of evidence obtained as a result of inadmissible confessions

If the confession has been excluded under s.76 or s.76A PACE:
- Any **evidence discovered as a result of the confession is** admissible;
- The fact that the evidence was discovered as a result of a confession is **not** admissible, **unless** D gives evidence (or it is given on his behalf) of how the evidence was obtained.

If the confession was excluded on another basis (e.g. s.78 PACE), the evidence discovered as a result of the confession will be admissible only if it passes the normal tests of relevance.

16.4 Making or challenging applications to exclude confessions

The objection to the confession should be made by representation to the judge **before the evidence is adduced** and in the absence of the jury. If the objection is raised after the confession has been adduced there is a common law power for the judge to:
- Direct the jury to ignore the evidence;
- Draw the jury's attention to matters which could affect the weight to be attached to the confession;
- Discharge the jury.

Excluding a confession adduced by P

Under **s.76(2)** PACE a confession can be excluded if it was obtained:
- By **oppression; or**
- In consequence of **anything said or done** which in the circumstances was likely to **render any confession made unreliable.**

Such evidence **must** be excluded unless P can prove **beyond reasonable doubt** that the confession was not obtained in the circumstances described above.

Examples of oppression include:
- Torture;
- Inhumane or degrading treatment;
- The use (or threat) of violence;
- The exercise of authority or power in a harsh or wrongful manner.

When considering the unreliability of a confession, **impropriety or bad faith is not required** before it can be excluded (although if the confession was obtained through impropriety, it almost certainly will be excluded).

A *voir dire* will be held and all parties will be given the opportunity to make representations. The court is not concerned with establishing whether the confession is true, but only with the circumstances in which it was obtained. A three-stage approach should be taken by the court:[89]

- Identify the thing said or done;
- Assess whether in the circumstances that thing was likely to have rendered the confession unreliable;
- Consider whether P has proved beyond reasonable doubt that the confession was not obtained in circumstances that render it unreliable.

The **PACE codes of practice** must be considered in any application to exclude the confession. But note that a **breach of a code does not automatically lead to the exclusion of evidence**. The relevant test is whether the breach is **significant** and **substantial**.

If D is mentally handicapped and his confession is admitted, the judge must warn the jury about the special need for caution before convicting him based on his confession.

Even where the confession would not be inadmissible under s.76 PACE, it may be excluded under:

- **s.78** PACE (see 16.5);
- The **common law power** to exclude evidence if its probative value is outweighed by the prejudice it will cause (see 10.4);
- s.126 of the CJA 2003, as hearsay (though this is really for the exclusion of evidence of little or no probative value; a confession will almost always be of probative value).

Excluding a confession adduced by a co-D

The test is the same as that for confessions adduced by P, i.e. if the confession was obtained:

- By **oppression**; or
- In consequence of **anything said or done** which in the circumstances was likely to **render any confession made unreliable**.

Such evidence must be excluded unless the co-D can prove **on the balance of probabilities** that the confession was not obtained in the circumstances described above.

---

[89] *R v Barry* (1991) 95 Cr App R 384.

The same considerations for oppression, unreliability and breaches of the PACE codes apply as described above for excluding a confession adduced by the prosecution.

It should be noted that there is no power to exclude this evidence under the common law or s.78 PACE, both of which apply only to P evidence.

16.5 The principles governing the exclusion of other prosecution evidence under s.78 of PACE

s.78 PACE gives the court discretion to exclude any P evidence if:

> "...it appears to the court that, having regard to all the circumstances, including the circumstances in which the evidence was obtained, the admission of the evidence would have **such an adverse effect on the fairness** of the proceedings that the court ought not to admit it".

The key test is whether its admission would make the proceedings **unfair**. s.78 PACE will normally be used to exclude evidence which has been obtained by an improper act or in bad faith, although its application is wide.

As to its relationship with the PACE codes, it should be noted that:
- A breach of the codes does not lead to automatic exclusion of the evidence;
- It is not necessary to find bad faith before evidence can be excluded under s.78 PACE.

16.6 Common categories of evidence that are the subject of applications to exclude under s.78 of PACE

s.78 PACE will commonly be used to exclude the following:
- Evidence obtained in breach of the PACE codes (e.g. failing to administer a caution or interviewing a juvenile without an appropriate adult being present);
- Evidence obtained through unlawful searches;
- Evidence obtained by trickery;
- Evidence obtained by unlawful eavesdropping;
- Evidence obtained by entrapment;
- Evidence obtained from D if he is mentally handicapped.

16.7 How to make or challenge applications to exclude evidence under s.78 of PACE

An application to exclude evidence under s.78 PACE should be made before the evidence is adduced and to the judge in the absence of the jury.

If it is sought to exclude evidence under s.78 PACE:
- A *voir dire* should be held for proceedings in the Crown Court;
- There is no requirement to hold a *voir dire* in a summary trial. However, if the Magistrates exclude evidence of D's pre-trial statements, they should seek the views of the parties as to whether the substantive hearing should be heard by a different bench.

17. Inferences from the Defendant's Conduct

17.1 The evidential significance of the defendant's lies

Evidence that D has told lies is **generally admissible** and will be **original evidence** not hearsay.

Such evidence can be used to **support evidence of guilt** and not just as merely reflecting on D's credibility.

The judge must usually give a **Lucas direction**[90] to the jury regarding lies if any of the below apply:
- D has raised an alibi;
- The judge has told the jury to look for supporting evidence such as lies;
- The prosecution is relying on the lie as evidence of guilt;
- There is a real danger the jury will rely on the lie.

The Lucas direction states that the lie can only support or strengthen evidence against D if it is:
- Deliberate; **and**
- Concerning a material issue; **and**
- Motivated by guilt or fear of the truth; **and**
- Shown to be untrue.

In addition the jury should be informed that:
- People lie for many reasons, such as shame or to bolster a just cause and not just from a sense of guilt;
- It must be sure beyond reasonable doubt that the statement is a lie, before it can use the statement as evidence of D's guilt.

17.2 The principles that apply to and potential consequences of the defendant's failure to mention facts when questioned

Under **s.34** CJPOA 1994, if **D fails to disclose a fact in questioning that he later relies upon in his defence** then an **adverse inference** may be drawn by:
- The court in determining if there is a case to answer;
- The court or jury in determining guilt.

An adverse inference =   The tribunal takes it into consideration against D when deciding guilt.

---

[90] *R v Lucas* [1981] QB 720.

It is not D's silence itself that triggers an adverse inference; it is **silence about a fact on which he later relies**. This means that no adverse inference will be drawn where D advances no positive case at trial and merely puts P to proof.

Also, generally no inference will be drawn if the fact on which D relies is shown to be true.

In the following circumstances the court can draw an adverse inference if D fails to disclose the facts of his defence:
- When being questioned under caution, **but before** being charged;
- Upon being charged.

Relying on a fact can include putting a specific positive case to a P witness.

The failure to mention the fact must be unreasonable. An inference should only be drawn if the **only** reason for D's failure to answer the question was that **he had no answer or none that would survive cross-examination**. Legal advice to keep silent may be a good reason not to have mentioned something (the jury will consider whether D *"genuinely and reasonably relied"* on that advice).

In order for an adverse inference to be drawn the following conditions must also have been complied with:
- The questions must have related to whether and by whom the offence was committed;
- The questioner must have been a constable or person with a duty to investigate offences;
- D must have been allowed legal advice (though he need not have taken it).

The judge should direct the jury that:
- D was not bound to answer the questions in interview;
- An inference from the silence cannot prove guilt on its own;
- P must have established a case to answer before any inference can be made;
- It is for the jury to decide if D could reasonably have answered the question;
- The inference can only be drawn if the jury is satisfied that D did not answer the question because **he did not have an answer to it or none that would survive cross-examination.**

17.3 The principles that apply to and potential consequences of the defendant's failure to account for objects, substances and marks

Under **s.36** CJPOA 1994, an adverse inference may be drawn if D fails to account for any **object, substance or mark** which is found:
- On his person;
- On his clothing;
- On his footwear;
- In his possession;
- At the place of arrest.

The court can draw an adverse inference as to:
- Whether D has a case to answer;
- Whether D is guilty.

The inference can only be drawn if:
- D was arrested by a constable (or customs and excise officer);
- D was informed of the consequences of a failure to explain;
- D had access to a solicitor if questioned in a place of authorised detention.

17.4 The principles that apply to and potential consequences of the defendant's failure to account for his presence at the scene of a crime

Under **s.37** CJPOA 1994, an adverse inference may be drawn if **D fails to account for his presence at the scene of a crime** at or about the time the offence was believed to have been committed.

The court can draw an adverse inference as to:
- Whether D has a case to answer;
- Whether D is guilty.

The inference can only be drawn if:
- D was arrested by a constable (or customs and excise officer);
- D was informed of the consequences of a failure to explain;
- D had access to a solicitor if questioned in a place of authorised detention.

17.5 The principles that apply to and potential consequences of the defendant's failure to testify in his own defence during the trial

Under **s.35** of the Criminal Justice and Public Order Act 1994, an **adverse inference** may be drawn if **D fails to testify in his own defence** unless:
- D's guilt is not in issue; **or**

- D has a mental or physical condition that makes testimony undesirable.

The court must satisfy itself that D is aware of the consequences of not giving evidence, or of giving evidence but refusing to answer a question.

The inference cannot be drawn where D's refusal to answer a question when giving evidence is because of:
- Legal privilege;
- A statute excluding the evidence in his answer;
- The court ruling that he should not answer.

The jury should be directed that:
- D has a right not to answer the question, but is aware that the jury may draw an adverse inference as a consequence;
- The failure to answer does not prove guilt, but it may assist in deciding guilt;
- If D has given a reason for not testifying which the jury accept then no inference can be drawn. However, if the jury does not accept the explanation the inference may be drawn;
- If they conclude that the only reason for D not testifying is that he had no answers or none that would survive cross-examination they may draw the adverse inference.

18. Identification Evidence

18.1 The special need for caution required in identification cases

There is a special need for caution in identification cases because there have been many miscarriages of justice based on identification evidence where multiple witnesses were mistaken. There is a risk of witnesses being convincing and sincere, but wrong nonetheless.

18.2 The circumstances in which a judge may withdraw an identification case from the jury

The trial judge should withdraw the case from the jury when the quality of the identifying evidence is **poor** and **unsupported**. An example of poor identification evidence is when the witness only had a fleeting glance. If the judge forms the view that the identifying evidence is poor and unsupported, he should invite submissions from the parties and if appropriate withdraw the case.

18.3 The nature and content of a Turnbull warning

In _**R v Turnbull**_,[91] the Court of Appeal provided these guidelines to be observed by judges in cases where the P case is **wholly or substantially** based upon the evidence of identification witnesses, and ID is in dispute.

1.   The jury should be warned of the need for special caution (see above). Mistaken witnesses can be convincing and a number of witnesses can be mistaken.

2.   The circumstances of the identification should be closely examined by the jury. The following factors will be relevant:
      - Length of time of the observation;
      - Distance from which observation was made;
      - Lighting conditions;
      - Any obstructions to the view;
      - Had the witness seen D before and if so how often or was there some special reason for remembering D?
      - Time between the initial observation and any subsequent identification procedure;
      - Any material discrepancy between the initial description given by the witness and the actual appearance of D.

---

[91] [1977] QB 224.

3.   Recognition is more reliable than identification, but even a witness who recognises someone can still be mistaken.

4.   If the quality of the identification evidence is good, the danger of mistaken identification is lessened and the jury can be left to assess its value. However, if the evidence is poor the case should be withdrawn from the jury and an acquittal directed. The judge should identify for the jury evidence which is capable of supporting the identification and evidence which is not.

5.   Care should be taken by the judge when directing the jury about the support for an identification which may be derived from the fact that they have rejected an alibi.

Content of a Turnbull direction

There is no special form of words for a Turnbull direction. However it should contain the following elements:
- An explanation that the case wholly or substantially relies on identification evidence which the defence disputes;
- A warning as to the special need for caution and the reasons for such caution;
- An explanation that a mistaken witness can be convincing and that a number of witnesses can be mistaken;
- A direction to examine closely the circumstances in which the identification was made;
- A reminder of any specific weaknesses in the identification (such as discrepancies between the initial description of D and D's actual appearance);
- A reminder that that mistaken recognition can occur, even with close friends and relatives;
- A highlight of the evidence that is capable of supporting the identification and the evidence which is not.

A Turnbull direction is not required when:
- There is no real question of mistaken identity (e.g. because D admits presence at the scene); or
- When the evidence given is of general characteristics (e.g. clothes) and would not identify a person; or
- When D alleges that the witness is lying about having identified D.

If the trial judge fails to give a Turnbull direction when one is required and D is convicted, the conviction will probably be quashed on appeal (though not necessarily, e.g. where the quality of the evidence is high or the risk of mistake was very low). Similarly, a defective Turnbull warning may also result in a conviction being quashed.

18.4 The grounds on which the judge might exclude identification evidence

ID evidence can be excluded under the common law or under s.78 PACE (see 16.5). Generally an application to exclude the evidence under PACE will be successful if the identification evidence is:
- Unreliable;
- Obtained in bad faith;
- Obtained in breach of a fundamental right.

A breach of the PACE code of practice for ID evidence (see Code D.3 of PACE at 2.3 above) does not automatically lead to the exclusion of the evidence, but may be an important consideration in deciding whether to exclude.

18.5 How to make or challenge applications to exclude identification evidence

In most cases counsel will make and challenge applications to exclude identification evidence by submissions to the judge in the absence of the jury. In rare circumstances it may be necessary to hold a *voir dire*.

If appropriate, at the close of the P case the defence may make a submission of no case to answer based on the fact that the evidence is poor and unsupported. If successful the judge will withdraw the case from the jury.

18.6 The circumstances in which the judge might warn the jury about *"suspect"* evidence

Generally there is **no need to warn the jury about the dangers of uncorroborated evidence** unless there is a statutory requirement or the **witness/evidence is *"suspect"***. A witness is suspect if he may **give unreliable evidence**.

Guidance on the approach to unreliable witnesses was given in ***R v Makanjuola***:[92]
- Warning the jury about the reliability of a witness is within the judge's discretion. Whether a warning is given and in what terms depends on the circumstances and issues of the case, as well as the content and quality of the evidence of the witness.
- It may be appropriate to warn the jury to exercise caution before acting on the unsupported evidence of a witness. There must be an evidential basis for suggesting unreliability and mere suggestion from cross-examination is not enough.
- The question of whether to give a special warning should be resolved in discussion before the final speeches and without the jury being present.

---

[92] [1995] 2 Crim App R 469.

- Where a warning is given, it should be as part of a review of the evidence and how to evaluate it, rather than as a set piece legal direction.
- It is for the judge to decide the strength and terms of the warning.
- The warning should not be used as an attempt to re-impose the former rules on corroboration.
- The Court of Appeal is disinclined to interfere with the judge's discretion, save in instances of *Wednesbury* unreasonableness.

19. Opinion Evidence and Experts

19.1 The general prohibition on the use of opinion evidence in criminal cases

In general, the **opinions of witnesses are not admissible** in criminal trials. It is for the court to form opinions and reach conclusions based on the evidence. There are two exceptions to this:

- An opinion on any matter that **does not call for expertise** and which is made as a way of conveying **facts personally perceived** by the witness is admissible evidence of what he perceived (e.g. *"D looked drunk"*); and
- **Expert evidence.**

19.2 The exception to the general rule in relation to expert evidence

An expert witness can offer an opinion when:

- The subject matter calls for expertise; **and**
- The witness has the requisite experience; **and**
- The subject matter of the opinion forms part of a body of knowledge or experience which is sufficiently organised or recognised to be accepted as a reliable body of knowledge or experience.

19.3 The definition of an expert

The key questions for determining whether someone can give expert evidence are:

- Does he have relevant expertise? Expertise doesn't necessarily mean qualifications, although expert witnesses will usually be highly qualified;
- Is he aware of his overriding duty to the court?
- Is he willing and able to fulfil that overriding duty to the court?

19.4 The scope and limits of expert evidence in the trial

Experts have the same status as any other witness and so it is for the jury to decide the weight that will be accorded to the expert's evidence. They are not bound by it.

The expert's opinions can be formed from:

- The facts in the case;
- Secondary facts (which are not considered to be hearsay) and include the expert's experience, as well as information from textbooks and academic journals.

By statute an **expert's report is not considered to be hearsay**. However, if the expert is not available to attend court, then the report can only be admitted as evidence with the court's permission.

The Court of Appeal has given the following guidance on expert evidence:
- It must be and be seen to be independent;
- The opinions expressed must be objective and unbiased;
- It must be made clear if any question is outside the expert's expertise;
- The facts and assumptions relied upon must be stated;
- It must be stated if there is insufficient data and so the opinion is only provisional;
- Experts may change their mind having exchanged reports with an expert instructed by another party.

An expert should also inform the court of any conflict of interest that arises.

19.5 The procedural requirements for the introduction of expert evidence

The CrimPR detail the process for introducing expert evidence. Any party wishing to introduce such evidence must **serve it on the court and every other party**, as soon as practicable, and in any event with any application relying on that evidence.

Once the expert evidence has been served, the serving party must on request give any other party a copy or reasonable opportunity to inspect:
- The record of any examination, measurement, test or experiment upon which the expert's opinions are based, or that were carried out in the course of reaching those opinions;
- Anything on which the examination, measurement, test or experiment was carried out.

If a party has not complied with the procedural requirements above, then it cannot introduce the expert evidence unless:
- All other parties agree; or
- The court gives permission.

The court can:
- Direct that the P and D experts should **prepare a joint statement.** The statement should detail the issues, including the areas of agreement and disagreement.
- **Exclude** the expert evidence of a party which has failed to comply with a direction for the experts to prepare such a statement.
- Direct the use of a **single joint expert** where more than one D wishes to introduce expert evidence.

The CrimPR also require that the report should state:

- The qualifications and relevant experience of the expert;
- The content of the instructions received;
- The questions asked of the expert;
- What material was provided;
- What has had a material effect on the expert's opinion;
- Who conducted any tests and the methods used;
- Any range of opinion on a matter;
- That the expert has complied with his duty to the court and that all parties will be notified if his opinion changes.

The report should also contain extracts from any relevant literature relied upon.

20. Privilege

20.1 The privilege against self-incrimination

D has **no obligation to incriminate himself** (= reveal a fact which renders it likely that proceedings will be commenced against him and expose him to a criminal charge or sanction).

This privilege extends to any situation where D has to provide oral evidence, documentation, information or any other item.

This type of privilege **does not** apply:
- If strong evidence against D already exists and so the evidence in question will not itself create a risk of proceedings being commenced;
- If the risk of proceedings can be avoided (e.g. by an undertaking from the DPP).

The privilege only applies to the person asserting it and evidence revealed without claiming privilege can be used in subsequent proceedings.

This type of privilege **does not protect D from answering questions relating to the proceedings in which he is currently involved** (if he refuses to answer questions relating to current proceedings, an adverse inference may be drawn against him – see 17.5)

There are many statutory exceptions to the privilege against self-incrimination. However, where an individual is obliged to answer questions, the relevant statute usually provides that his answers cannot be used in criminal proceedings against him for that offence. This protects the principle behind the privilege against self-incrimination

20.2 The principles that apply to legal professional privilege

There are 2 types of legal professional privilege (**LPP**):
- **Legal Advice Privilege**: attaching to communications between D and his lawyer made for the purpose of giving legal advice. The privilege applies whether or not litigation is contemplated.

- **Litigation Privilege**: attaching to communications between D and his lawyers regarding any litigation or pending litigation.

For both types, privilege will only attach where the communications were:
- **Confidential; and**

113

- Created for the **dominant purpose** of obtaining legal advice or conducting litigation (the "***dominant purpose test***"). Communications made for a different reason, or for an additional reason of equal importance, will not be privileged.

Privilege can also extend to communications with a third party (e.g. an expert), as long as the dominant purpose test is satisfied.

LPP can be waived but **only by D** (never by his lawyers). If privilege is waived D's lawyer can be cross-examined about the advice given.

There are limits and exceptions to this type of privilege:
- Documents are not privileged just because they are held by D's lawyer;
- Communications made to further a criminal or fraudulent purpose are not privileged;
- Privilege attaches to communications between D and his lawyer, not to facts perceived between them (e.g. D's identity or that D sought legal advice);
- Privilege attaches to the communications themselves and not the facts contained within: if that information becomes available to P by some other means the privilege is lost.

Section 4

Cases involving youths

21. Youth Courts

21.1 The categorisation of youths into *"child"* and *"young person"* and its legal consequences

Anybody under the age of 18 is considered a youth. Youths are categorised as follows (but note that these categories only really make a difference at sentencing):

- A person **aged 14-17** is considered a **young person**;
- A person **aged 10-13** is considered a **child**;
- A person under the age of 10 is **irrebuttably incapable of crime**, and cannot be prosecuted.

21.2 The diversion of youths from the criminal justice system by the use of reprimands and warnings (outline only)

When a youth commits an offence or is suspected of doing so, the police have three options:

- Charge Youth-D;
- Offer Youth-D a **reprimand**;
- Offer Youth-D a **warning**.

Reprimands and warnings are alternatives to prosecution, akin to cautions offered to adults. A reprimand is usually offered for the first offence, and a warning for the second or for a more serious first offence.

A reprimand or warning can only be given when:

- There is a realistic prospect of conviction on the evidence available; and
- Youth-D admits committing the offence; and
- Youth-D has no previous convictions; and
- It is not in the public interest to prosecute;

AND

For a reprimand:	For a warning:

• Youth-D has not previously received a reprimand or warning; and
• The offence is not serious enough to merit a warning.
	• Youth-D has received no warnings before; or
	• Youth-D has received one warning but:
	  ◦ The warning was given more than 2 years ago; and
	  ◦ The offence is not serious enough to merit a charge.

Only one reprimand can ever be given, and only a maximum of two warnings.

The Youth Court is effectively a specialist Magistrates' Court, and the procedure closely mirrors that of the Magistrates' Court. However, there are some key differences.

The tribunal comprises 3 Magistrates (or a district judge), at least **one of whom should be a woman and at least one of whom should be a man.** A single-sex tribunal is permitted only when:
- The situation could not have been foreseen; and
- It is in interests of justice not to adjourn to wait for a mixed-sex tribunal.

If Youth-D is aged 15 or younger, his parent **must** attend, and can be compelled to do so. If Youth-D is aged 16-17, his or her parent **may** attend. A parent should also attend if the court intends to make a parenting order. The parent will sit beside Youth-D.

As in the Magistrates' Court, wigs and gowns are not worn in the Youth Court. Juvenile witnesses will receive special measures (see 13.4). Note:
- Those under 17 are presumed to need special measures, although may refuse them;
- Those over 17 are not presumed to need them, but may request them.

The media may report from the Youth Court, but **the media are banned from reporting any details which may identify any child or young person involved in a case in the Youth Court.**[93] The ban can be lifted:
- When D applies to lift the ban. This happens where publicity is appropriate for the avoidance of injustice to D (e.g. to try to locate defence witnesses).

- When P applies to lift the ban. This happens where:
    - The juvenile is *"unlawfully at large"*; and
    - Publicity may assist in his recapture; and
    - The offence is serious (maximum punishment of 14+ years for an adult offender) or violent or sexual (as defined in Schedule 15 CJA 2003).

- After conviction of D, if the Youth Court considers the lifting of reporting restrictions to be in the public interest.

There is **no general public right to enter a youth courtroom.** Those permitted to enter are:[94]
- Youth-D himself;
- Youth-D's parents;
- The parties' legal representatives;

---

[93] s.49 CYPA 1933.
[94] s.47(2) CYPA 1933.

- The Magistrates / judge;
- Court officers;
- Bona fide media reporters;
- Witnesses (during or after giving evidence);
- Anyone else directly concerned in the case (e.g. probation officers and social workers);
- Such other persons as specially authorised by the court.

A Youth-D will be addressed by his first name.

A Youth-D who is a young person (i.e. 14-17) will not swear an oath before giving evidence, but instead will **promise to tell the truth**. A child (i.e. 13 or under) will give evidence unsworn.

Technically, a Youth-D is not *"convicted"*, he has a *"finding of guilt"* made against him. However, much of the legislation and the sentencing guidelines refer to *"convictions"*.

21.4 The circumstances in which a youth will appear in the adult Magistrates' Court and in the Crown Court, including how the dangerous offender provisions apply to youths

The usual method of classifying offences (into summary, either-way and indictable offences) does not apply to youths. **A youth must be tried summarily in the Youth Court**, except in four instances:

1. He is charged **jointly with an adult,** and the court considers it **necessary in the interests of justice** for them to be tried together.[95]

2. He is charged with a **homicide** offence (in which case he will be tried in the Crown Court).

3. He may require a **sentence of long-term detention**.[96] The court must be satisfied that:
   - The offence is a *"grave"* one (i.e. an adult D would face 14+ years' imprisonment, or it is a specified sexual or firearms offence);[97] and
   - It may require a sentence of long-term detention; and
   - There is a real prospect of a sentence of two or more years' detention being imposed.

---

[95] s.24 MCA 1980.
[96] s.24(1)(a) MCA 1980.
[97] s.91 PCC(S)A 2000.

4.   He may need to be sentenced as a **dangerous offender** (see chapter 26).

The definition of a dangerous offender is the same for youths as for adults (*"there is a significant risk to members of the public of serious harm occasioned by the commission by him of further specified offences"*), but slightly different provisions apply to dangerous offender youths:

- A life sentence **must** be imposed where:[98]
    - Youth-D is convicted of a *"serious offence"* (see 26.1); and
    - Youth-D is a dangerous offender; and
    - Youth-D is liable to receive a life sentence under s.91 PCC(S)A 2000; and
    - The seriousness of his offence is such that a life sentence is justified.

- An extended sentence **may** be imposed where:[99]
    - Youth-D is a dangerous offender; and
    - The court is not required to impose a life sentence under the provision above; and
    - The court would sentence Youth-D to at least 4 years' custody.

21.5 The sentences available to the Youth Court

Two sentences are the same as those available in the (adult) Magistrates' Courts:
- An absolute or conditional discharge;
- A fine (note that where Youth-D is under 16, the fine is the responsibility of Youth-D's parent).

Sentences unique to the Youth Court are:
- A Referral Order;
- A Youth Rehabilitation Order;
- A Detention and Training Order (DTO).

When determining a sentence for a Youth-D, the court will not apply the same sentencing principles as for adults (see 22.7). The court need not directly consider the need to reduce crime by deterrence, but it should have regard to:
- The principal aim of the youth justice system (= to prevent reoffending);[100]
- The welfare of Youth-D.

Unlike with adults, the court also need not necessarily treat every previous conviction as an aggravating factor (although it may do so).

---

[98] s.226 CJA 2003.
[99] s.226B CJA 2003.
[100] s.142A CJA 2003.

Referral Order

There is no real equivalent to a Referral Order in the adult courts: it is a uniquely youth sentence.[101] Youth-D will be referred to a Youth Offending Team (YOT), will sign a *"youth offender contract"* making certain commitments, and he will attend meetings with a Youth Offending Panel made up of two members of the local community and an adviser from the YOT.

A Referral Order will last **from 3 to 12 months.**

A Referral Order is:[102]

- **Mandatory** if Youth-D pleads guilty to all offences for which he is before the court and has never previously been convicted (unless it is not in the interests of justice to impose one);
- **Discretionary** if the mandatory conditions are not met, which will be because either:
  - Youth-D has previously been convicted; and/or
  - Youth-D is being dealt with for 2 or more offences, and he pleads guilty to at least one of those offences (but not to all).

The court **may not make any other sentence** when it makes a referral order. A Referral Order is also not available when Youth-D faces a mandatory sentence fixed by law.

Youth Rehabilitation Order (YRO)

A Youth Rehabilitation Order (YRO) is the youth equivalent of a Community Order. It will be made where:[103]

- The offence is serious enough to warrant a YRO; and
- The restriction of liberty is proportionate to the offence.

There are many requirements that can be attached to a YRO (more than can be attached to an adult Community Order). Some of the most common are:

- Supervision;
- Unpaid Work (where Youth-D is 16-17);
- Activity Requirement or Prohibited Activity Requirement;
- Curfew;
- Drug Treatment or Testing;
- Residence at a particular address, or residence with the Local Authority;
- Attendance Centre Requirement.

---

[101] See ss.16-32 PCC(S)A 2000.
[102] s.17 PCC(S)A 2000.
[103] ss.147-148 CJA 2003.

The maximum length of a YRO is **three years.** The court cannot sentence Youth-D to a YRO if he is subject to one already (unlike with adult Community Orders, which can run concurrently).

Breach of the requirements of a YRO will be dealt with in a similar way to breach of an adult Community Order (see 23.5). However, Youth-D must breach his requirements **three times** before breach proceedings are initiated (rather than twice, as for adults). Upon finding that Youth-D has breached the requirements of a YRO, the court can:

- Take no action;
- Fine Youth-D (where Youth-D is under 16, the fine is the responsibility of his parents);
- Amend the YRO (with some restrictions);
- Revoke the YRO and re-sentence Youth-D to any sentence appropriate for the original offence.

Detention and Training Order (DTO)

A Detention and Training Order (DTO) is the equivalent of a custodial sentence in the adult courts. It means that Youth-D will go to a young offenders' institution (= youth prison). It can only be made when:

- The **custody threshold has been passed**; and
- The maximum sentence for an adult convicted of the same offence would be **at least 4 months**.

DTO and Age

A DTO is available for defendants aged **12 to 17 at the date of conviction**.

If Youth-D is aged **15-17**, there are no additional restrictions on imposing a DTO.

If Youth-D is aged **12-14**, a DTO may **only** be imposed if:
- He is a **persistent offender; or**
- The offence is specified in **s.91 PCC(S)A 2000** (i.e. for an adult it would be punishable with 14 years' custody or more, **or** it is an offence specified in s.91 itself).

If Youth-D is aged **10-11, he cannot receive a DTO**. If he must be imprisoned, it must be under s.91 PCC(S)A 2000, and the sentence can only be imposed by the Crown Court.

A DTO may **only** be of these lengths: **4, 6, 8, 10, 12, 18, or 24** months. For summary offences, a DTO must not be longer than 6 months.[104]

Youth-D who receives a DTO is in detention for **half the term**, and on release is placed under a **supervision requirement** for the rest of the order.

If Youth-D fails to comply with the supervision requirement under a DTO, the court can:
- Impose a fine; or
- Return him to custody for a maximum of 3 months.

If the offence falls within the scope of s.91 PCC(S)A 2000, even a 24-month DTO may be too lenient. In that case, the court's sentencing powers are increased to those applicable to an adult.

Where Youth-D is convicted in an adult court

Where Youth-D is convicted in an adult court, the adult court **must**, unless undesirable to do so, remit the case to the appropriate Youth Court for sentence. However, where the adult court is a Magistrates' Court, this does not apply where:
- Youth-D must be sentenced to a mandatory referral order; or
- Youth-D can properly be sentenced to an absolute or conditional discharge, a fine, or an order requiring his parent to enter into a recognizance to take proper control of him.[105]

In these circumstances, the adult Magistrates' Court **may** remit the case to the Youth Court, but does not have to.

---

[104] See s.101 PCC(S)A 2000.
[105] s.8(7) and (8) PCC(S)A 2000.

Section 5

Sentencing

22. Sentencing Principles

22.1 The sentencing powers of the Magistrates' Court and the Crown Court (including the power to sentence youths)

Magistrates' Court

The Magistrates' Court has the power to sentence for any offence which has been tried in the Magistrates' Court (i.e. summary only offences and either-way offences which have been tried summarily). The Magistrates' Court is limited to the statutory maximum for each offence when tried summarily, and in any case can only pass the following sentences:

- Custodial: **up to 6 months in total**, or 12 months total if awarding consecutive sentences for multiple either-way offences;
- Community Order;
- Fine: **up to £5,000;**
- Conditional discharge;
- Absolute discharge.

In determining sentence, the Magistrates will have regard to the **Magistrates' Court Sentencing Guideline**, which provides guidelines for every offence which may appear before the court. Where the Magistrates try an either-way offence and, having convicted, feel that their sentencing powers would be too low (i.e. a custodial term of more than 6 months or a fine of more than £5,000 is warranted), they can **commit D to the Crown Court** to be sentenced.[106]

Crown Court

The Crown Court can sentence for any offence which has been tried in the Crown Court (i.e. indictable-only offences and either-way offences which have been tried in the Crown Court). There are no maximum limits on custodial sentences and fines (so the Crown Court can impose a life sentence or any fine), although it must not pass a sentence which exceeds the statutory maximum for that offence.

It can also sentence those who have been committed to the Crown Court for sentence by the Magistrates' Court. Note that when the Crown Court is hearing an appeal against conviction from the Magistrates' Court, its sentencing powers are limited to those of the Magistrates' Court.

---

[106] ss.3-5 PCC(S)A 2000.

In respect of Detention and Training Orders (see 21.5), the powers of the Youth Court and the Crown Court are identical.

Under s. 91 PCC(S)A 2000, the Crown Court may impose a sentence of **long-term detention** on a Youth-D (the maximum sentence being the same as for adult) where either:
- The offence is punishable with 14 years' imprisonment or more; or
- The offence is specified in s.91 itself.

However, such a sentence can only be used where Youth-D is convicted in the Crown Court.

22.2 Sentencing procedure in the Magistrates' Court

The Magistrates can either:
- Sentence D immediately following his conviction / guilty plea (usually when the offence is only punishable by a fine, or a custodial sentence is inevitable and the court sees no need for a Probation report); or
- Adjourn the matter for reports.

Where the Magistrates are considering passing a custodial sentence (including a suspended sentence order with conditions) or a community penalty, they need to hear the opinion of the Probation Service.[107] The Probation Service will interview D and assess his suitability for a community penalty and what conditions might be appropriate; they will then write a **Pre-Sentence Report** (PSR) in which they make a recommendation to the Court. The Magistrates are not obliged to follow this recommendation.

An adjournment for a PSR usually lasts **3 weeks**. D can be released on bail or kept in custody.

The court can also postpone sentencing when, for example, there are multiple Ds and it is desirable for them to be sentenced together, or where D faces several outstanding charges and should be sentenced for them all together.

Sentencing will proceed as follows:

1.   P will open the facts of the offence (this will not happen where D has just been convicted after a trial and sentencing takes place immediately, as the Magistrates will already be familiar with the facts).

---

[107] s.156 CJA 2003.

2.   P will provide the court with a copy of D's antecedents (= previous convictions).

3.   P may apply for its costs from D.

4.   D will be allowed to mitigate (see 22.9 for common mitigating features) and make representations on costs, if applicable.

5.   The Magistrates will pass sentence, sometimes after a period of retirement to consider the appropriate sentence.

22.3 Sentencing procedure in the Crown Court, including committals for sentence

Sentencing procedure in the Crown Court is essentially the same as in the Magistrates' Court.

Where the Magistrates try an either-way offence and, having convicted, feel that their sentencing powers would be too low (i.e. a custodial term of more than 6 months or a fine of more than £5,000 is warranted), they can **commit D to the Crown Court** to be sentenced.[108]

22.4 Determining the facts of the offence, including Newton hearings, the use of a basis of plea and pre-sentence reports

Where D is convicted after a trial, the Magistrates or the judge can determine the facts of the offence (consistent with the jury's verdict), and sentence accordingly.

It is always open to D to plead guilty but put forward a **basis of plea,** where he disagrees with one part of the P case. For example, if D is accused of assault by beating on the basis that he punched V three times, he may plead guilty but on the basis that he only punched V once. P will either accept this basis (in which case D will be sentenced on the version of events presented in his basis of plea), or reject it and there may be a **Newton hearing**.

A Newton hearing is essentially a trial (often shorter than a real trial because much is already agreed) in which the Magistrates/judge determine whose version of events is to be accepted.

P bears the burden of proof in a Newton hearing, and the standard of proof is **beyond reasonable doubt.**

---

[108] ss.3-5 PCC(S)A 2000.

It is the responsibility of D's counsel to alert the court to the need for a Newton hearing.

There is no need to hold a Newton hearing where:
- The dispute is immaterial to sentence (in which case the court will take D's version);
- D's version is implausible;
- D's contention does not contradict the P case.

Sometimes it will be more appropriate to add an additional charge to the indictment and empanel a jury to decide the dispute.

A PSR will also contain an outline of D's version of the facts, as presented to the Probation Officer. If D in his PSR presents a version of events materially different from P's, the sentencing judge will not usually have regard to it, although if D wishes to be sentenced on the basis on the facts as put forward in his PSR, the issue will have to be resolved by calling evidence.[109]

22.5 Indications as to sentence

A judge can, on request, give an **indication of the maximum sentence** he would pass if a guilty plea were entered immediately. This is called a **Goodyear indication.**[110] The agreed basis of plea should be given in writing, and the hearing requesting a Goodyear indication should take place in open court. A Goodyear indication is normally sought at the PCMH.

The judge has an unfettered discretion to refuse to give a Goodyear indication, or to wait for any reason (e.g. until a report is prepared). It is also generally inappropriate to ask for a Goodyear indication where there is any material dispute between P and D as to the facts on which D might be convicted.

Once given, **a Goodyear indication is binding on everyone.** However, any sentence passed following a Goodyear indication can still be referred to the Court of Appeal as unduly lenient.

A Goodyear indication ceases to have effect after a **reasonable opportunity to plead guilty has passed.**

---

[109] *R v Tolera* [1999] 1 Cr App R (S) 25.
[110] *R v Goodyear* [2005] EWCA Crim 888.

22.6 The role of prosecuting counsel in sentence

P's role at sentence is to:
- Open the facts (where necessary);
- Outline any aggravating and mitigating factors disclosed by the P case;
- State any statutory provisions relevant to the offender (e.g. that he is currently subject to a conditional discharge or to a minimum sentence);
- Draw the court's attention to the relevant sentencing guidelines and/or guideline case law;
- Put forward the views of V, where relevant;
- Make appropriate applications for costs, compensation or other ancillary orders.

P's role is **not** to advocate for a harsher sentence. P is effectively **neutral at sentence**.

Where D is unrepresented and P knows of personal mitigation relevant to D, P should make sure the court is aware of it. Where D is represented, personal mitigation is the role of D's representative.

22.7 The purposes of sentence

When sentencing adults, the sentencing principles to be applied are to:[111]
- Punish offenders;
- Reduce crime by deterrence;
- Reform and rehabilitate offenders;
- Protect the public;
- Provide reparation to victims.

For youths, the court need not directly consider the need to reduce crime by deterrence, but it should have regard to:
- The principal aim of the youth justice system (to prevent reoffending);
- The welfare of Youth-D.

---

[111] s.142 CJA 2003.

Seriousness is determined by examining D's **culpability,** and the **degree of harm** D caused.[112]

Seriousness = culpability + harm

The level of seriousness of an offence will:
- Determine which (if any) sentencing thresholds have been crossed;
- Indicate what type of sentence is appropriate (i.e. custodial, community or other);
- Determine the onerousness of the sentence.

There are four basic levels of culpability:
- **Intention;**
- **Recklessness;**
- **Knowledge;**
- **Negligence.**

Harm can be caused to:
- The direct victim of the offence;
- To the community as a whole;
- Other, e.g. indirectly to an individual.

There are some statutory aggravating factors to which the court must have regard in all cases when sentencing. They are that the:
- Offence was committed while on bail for other offences;
- Offence was racially or religiously aggravated;
- Offence was motivated by, or demonstrates, hostility based on the victim's sexual orientation (or presumed sexual orientation);
- Offence was motivated by, or demonstrates, hostility based on the victim's disability (or presumed disability);
- Offender has previous convictions that the court considers can reasonably be treated as aggravating factors having regard to their relevance to the current offence and the time that has elapsed since conviction.

---

[112] s.143(1) CJA 2003.

Common aggravating factors

Aside from the statutory aggravating factors, the **court will then consider all other factors relevant to the offence or to D**. The factors listed below are not exhaustive, but are intended to be a sample. The court must be careful not to double-count, i.e. where something is an element of the offence, it cannot also constitute an aggravating or mitigating factor (e.g. racially aggravated assault).[113]

Relevant to culpability	Relevant to harm
<ul><li>Intention to cause more serious harm than actually resulted</li><li>Offence was planned</li><li>Offence involved an abuse or power or abuse of a position of trust</li><li>Professional offending</li><li>Operating in a group</li><li>Use of a weapon</li><li>Under the influence of drink or drugs at the time of the offence</li></ul>	<ul><li>Multiple victims</li><li>Offence had a particularly serious effect on the victim</li><li>Vulnerable victim (e.g. child)</li><li>Sustained assault on the victim</li><li>Victim is a public sector worker acting in the course of duty</li><li>Presence of others during offence</li></ul>

Common mitigating factors

Relevant to culpability	Relevant to harm
<ul><li>Greater degree of provocation than normal</li><li>D suffers from mental illness or disability</li><li>D's young age</li><li>minor role of D</li><li>No planning of offence</li><li>Prompt surrender</li></ul>	<ul><li>Offence caused little damage</li><li>Property restored to owner</li><li>No injury or less significant injury in the context of the offence</li></ul>

Guilty plea

A **guilty plea is a significant mitigating factor** and will attract a **discount in sentence**. The sentencing judge must take into account the stage at which the guilty plea was entered, and the circumstances in which it was entered.[114]

---

[113] s. 29 CDA 1998.
[114] s.144 CJA 2003.

There is a sliding scale of reduction for a guilty plea:

- ⅓ **discount** for a guilty plea at the earliest opportunity;
- ¼ **discount** for a guilty plea at the PCMH or where the trial date has already been set;
- ¹⁄₁₀ **discount** for a guilty plea on the day of trial or after the trial has begun.

The judge may depart from this sliding scale in appropriate circumstances, such as where the evidence against D is overwhelming. In such circumstances, a reduction of ⅕ for a guilty plea at the earliest opportunity would be appropriate. The judge may also award full credit even where D has not pleaded guilty at the earliest opportunity, such as where it was not reasonable to expect D to enter a plea at the earliest opportunity because evidence had not been served.

A guilty plea can also alter the kind of sentence passed (e.g. passing a non-custodial sentence even where custody threshold has been passed).

Where there is a Newton hearing (see 22.4) and D's version of events is rejected, this is taken into account in determining the level of reduction in sentence. Some reduction for a guilty plea will normally be given, but the sentencer is entitled to give no discount at all where this is appropriate.

How a sentence is determined

1. Determine the offence seriousness (and so its *"category"*) and therefore the starting point by looking only at the statutory aggravating and mitigating factors for that offence.

2. Move up or down from the starting point based on other aggravating and mitigating factors. Consider also D's personal mitigation.

3. Reduction for assisting P, if relevant.

4. Reduction for a guilty plea.

5. Dangerousness.

6. Totality – where D is being sentenced for more than one offence, the overall sentence must reflect D's overall criminality.

7. Consider compensation and other ancillary orders.

22.10 Custody and community sentence thresholds

The court may **only** impose a sentence of imprisonment where the custody threshold has been met, i.e. that the offence or the combination of associated offences is **so serious that neither a fine alone nor a community sentence can be justified for the offence** (see 24.1).[115]

Similarly, the court may **only** impose a community sentence where the community sentence threshold has been met. This threshold is that the offence or the combination of associated offences was **serious enough to warrant such a sentence**.

22.11 The purpose of the Sentencing Council and how it issues guidance for the courts, including the importance of Court of Appeal guideline cases

The Sentencing Council issues sentencing guidelines which the courts should follow when determining sentence. This is to ensure consistency, i.e. that sentences are roughly uniform wherever and by whomever they are imposed.

Guidelines do not exist for every offence. Even where guidelines exist, the court can depart from them where appropriate.

The sentencing court can also consider Court of Appeal guideline cases, i.e. cases when a sentence has been appealed by either P or D, and the Court of Appeal has determined the correct approach to sentencing for that particular offence.

Court of Appeal cases are particularly important when there are no sentencing guidelines.

---

[115] s.152(2) CJA 2003.

23. Non-custodial Sentences

23.1 Principles for the imposition of absolute and conditional discharges

An absolute discharge = **D receives no punishment**, although he will still have a criminal record.[116] An absolute discharge will be imposed where the court decides that it is inappropriate to inflict any punishment on D (e.g. where D is guilty in law, but virtually or entirely blameless).

A conditional discharge = **D is discharged on condition that he does not commit a further offence** in a period specified by the Court.[117] That period can be **up to 3 years**. If D does commit a further offence in that period, he can be re-sentenced for the initial offence, in addition to being sentenced for the further offence.

23.2 Principles relevant to the imposition of a fine, including the consequences of default

Fines in the Magistrates' Court fall into five levels ranging from £200 to £5,000.[118]

Fines can also be divided into bands based on a percentage of D's relevant weekly income, ranging from 25% to 500%; e.g. an offence may be punishable by a *"Band C fine"*.

In fining D, the court will proceed through these 3 stages:
- Decide what fine is appropriate in light of the seriousness of the offence;
- Reduce it in response to mitigation or an early guilty plea;
- Adjust it to reflect the financial circumstances of D.

The total fine should usually be an amount that D can pay within 12 months.

To assist in the third stage, the court can make a **financial circumstances order** requiring D to outline his financial means.

If D has been remanded in custody but is eventually sentenced to a fine, the fine should be reduced to reflect the time spent in custody.

---

[116] s.12(1)(a) PCC(S)A 2000.
[117] s.12(1)(b) PCC(S)A 2000.
[118] s.37(2) CJA 1982.

Payment of the fine is due immediately, although the court can grant time to pay and/or permission to pay in instalments.

In the Magistrates' Court: the maximum fine that the Magistrates can impose is £5,000 per offence, up to a maximum of £25,000 for five offences. The Magistrates may impose a **sentence in default** (= custodial sentence that D will serve if he doesn't pay his fine) in certain circumstances.[119]

In the Youth Court:
- Where D is aged 15-17, the maximum fine that the Youth Court can impose is £1000;
- Where D is aged 10-14, the maximum fine that the Youth Court can impose is £250.

Where D is aged under 16, D's parents **must** pay. If D is aged 16-17, D's parents **may** pay.

In the Crown Court: the court can impose a fine **instead of or in addition to** dealing with D in any other way.[120] This applies whether D was committed for sentence from the Magistrates' Court, or convicted in Crown Court. The Crown Court **must** also impose a *"sentence in default"*.[121]

Enforcement of a fine is carried out **by D's local Magistrates' Court**. If D fails to pay, the Magistrates can issue a summons or a warrant for D's arrest. At a subsequent hearing, it will investigate D's means. The court may remit (= cancel) the fine in whole or in part at any time if there has been a change of D's circumstances and it would be fair to do so,[122] or it may enforce the fine.

The court has a variety of enforcement methods:
- Deduction from benefits;
- Attachment of earnings order (= money deducted automatically from D's earnings);
- Distress warrant (= authorising seizure and sale of D's goods);
- Attendance centre order (if D is under 25);
- Unpaid work/curfew requirement;
- Imprisonment.

A term of imprisonment may be fixed only if:

---

[119] s.82 MCA 1980.
[120] s.163 CJA 2003.
[121] s.139 PCC(S)A 2000.
[122] s.85(1) MCA 1980.

- The offence is punishable by imprisonment **and** D has the means to pay immediately; **or**
- Enforcement of the fine by other methods is likely to be impossible because D is transient.

Fines can also be increased in the event of non-payment.[123]

23.3 Principles for the imposition of a community sentence, including the objectives of such sentences

A community sentence (or community penalty) = **a sentence that will be served in the community.**[124] D is at liberty, but will usually have to attend appointments with the Probation Service for a certain amount of time, and abide by any other requirements imposed as part of a community order (e.g. unpaid work).

A community sentence can **only** be imposed if:
- The community sentence **threshold has been crossed**[125] (see 22.10); and
- The offence is punishable with imprisonment, unless D has been fined more than 3 times.[126]

The court must ensure that the order is both suitable for the offender and commensurate with the seriousness of the offence.

The **maximum duration of a community order is 3 years**.

The objectives of community sentences – in addition to the usual objectives which apply to all sentences – are to allow D to make amends to his community and to allow him to rehabilitate in the community. Community penalties counter some of the negative effects of custody (e.g. exposing D to more serious criminals, and institutionalising D).

The court should generally obtain a PSR before imposing a community sentence unless it decides that one is unnecessary.

When passing sentence, the court should make clear whether credit has been given and its reasons if it does not do so.

---

[123] Sch.5 Courts Act 2003.
[124] See also ss.147 and 177 CJA 2003.
[125] s.148(1) CJA 2003.
[126] s.150A CJA 2003.

There is only one broad type of community sentence: a **community order**.[127] However, the court can select from a wide range of requirements to impose as part of a community order to construct an appropriate sentence.[128]

These can be remembered using the mnemonic **UP SPACE DRAMA:**

Unpaid work
Programme

Supervision
Prohibited activity
Activity requirement
Curfew
Exclusion

Drug rehabilitation
Residence
Alcohol treatment
Mental health treatment
Attendance centre (where D aged under 25)

The court must consider whether the requirements are compatible with one another (and with D's religious beliefs, ordinary commitments, etc).

23.5 Consequences of breach of a community sentence

If the probation officer considers that **without reasonable excuse** D has failed to comply with any term of a community order, the officer must **give D a warning** or, if the breach is particularly serious, send it straight back to court to be dealt with. If, within 12 months, D again fails to comply the officer **must** send the case back to the court for the breach to be dealt with.[129]

Breach of a community order must be proved **beyond reasonable doubt.** The court can then either:
- **Amend** the order to impose **more onerous** requirements; or
- **Revoke** the order and pass no new sentence; or
- **Revoke** the order and **re-sentence** in any way that it could have sentenced the original offence; or
- Impose a sentence of **imprisonment of 6 months**, although only where:

---

[127] s.147 CJA 2003.
[128] s.177 CJA 2003.
[129] See generally sch.8 CJA 2003.

- o   D is aged 18 or more; and
- o   the initial offence was not punishable with imprisonment; and
- o   D has wilfully and persistently failed to comply.

Breaches of orders imposed by the Magistrates' Court will be dealt with in the Magistrates' Court, and breaches of orders imposed by the Crown Court will be dealt with in the Crown Court. However, a Crown Court can stipulate at the time of sentence that any breaches will be dealt with in the Magistrates' Court, and the Magistrates can commit D to the Crown Court.

When dealing with a breach of a community order, the court must bear in mind the following guidelines:

- The primary objective is to ensure that the original requirements are completed;
- The court **must** take into account the extent to which D has complied with the requirements;
- Custody should be the last resort;
- Before imposing more onerous requirements, the court should consider D's ability to comply;
- It may be necessary to re-sentence to a community order with different requirements.

Community orders can be revoked for reasons other than breach, such as where D is making good progress, or falls ill. Likewise, the court may amend the community order **on the application of D or a responsible officer**. The court may:

- Cancel any requirement;
- Replace a requirement with one of the same kind that was open to it when initially making the order;
- Adjust a requirement.

The court **cannot make an order of a completely different kind**.

Drug rehabilitation and alcohol treatment requirements cannot be modified without D's consent; if D refuses consent, the court can revoke the order and re-sentence D.

If a community order in force is when D is convicted of another offence in the Magistrates' Court, the Magistrates may, if it is in the interests of justice:

- Revoke the order;
- Revoke the order and re-sentence D for the offence in respect of which the order was made;
- Deal with D in any way in which D could have originally been sentenced.

A binding over order = making someone promise to be of good behaviour or keep the peace. A court can also bind over the parent/guardian of a youth as an ancillary order to a youth sentence.

Being bound over is not a conviction. In some instances, the person being bound over will pay a surety, which will be forfeited if he does not keep the peace.

24. Custodial Sentences

24.1 Requirements before a custodial sentence can be passed

The **custody threshold must be crossed** before a custodial sentence can be passed.[130] This threshold is that the offence or combination of offences is:

> **So serious that neither a fine alone nor a community sentence can be justified for the offence**

Custody can also be imposed if D fails to express his willingness to comply with a requirement proposed by the court to be included in the community order which requires an expression of such willingness.

In borderline cases, the court will take into account factors such as:
- D's admission of responsibility, particularly if at the earliest opportunity and accompanied by remorse;
- D's genuine self-motivated determination to address his addiction/behaviour etc;
- D's youth and immaturity;
- D's previous good character and the fact that he has never been in prison before.

Any custodial sentence **must** be as short as possible.

24.2 Concurrent and consecutive sentences, including the totality principle

Where D is sentenced to multiple sentences of imprisonment, those sentences will generally run:
- Concurrently (= at the same time) if they are in respect of a single series of incidents;
- Consecutively (= one after the other) if they are in respect of unrelated or clearly separate offences.

The **totality principle** is that when sentencing for more than a single offence the total sentence must reflect all of the offending behaviour and be just and proportionate. It is usually impossible to achieve this by adding together the notional single sentences.[131]

---

[130] s.152(2) CJA 2003.
[131] Sentencing Council Guideline – Offences Taken into Consideration and Totality.

A custodial term of **between 14 days and 2 years** may be suspended.[132]

A suspended sentence order (SSO) is made where the custody threshold has been passed and D is sentenced to custody, but D is not sent to prison. D remains at liberty unless he:

- **Fails to comply with any requirement** of his SSO during the **supervisional** period; and/or
- **Commits further offences** during the **operational** period.

All SSOs have a stated **operational period**. This is the amount of time for which the sentence is suspended.

A judge **may** also make requirements as part of an SSO, e.g. unpaid work. If so, then the SSO will have a **supervision period**. This is the amount of time for which D must comply with the requirements of his SSO.

There is no obligation on the judge to impose requirements.

The operational period (and supervision period, if requirements are imposed) must be specified by the court. Both have to be **between 6 months and 2 years.** The operational period must be **the same length or longer** than the supervision period.

> *For example: D receives a sentence of 9 months' imprisonment suspended for 2 years. As part of his SSO, he must undergo a period of 12 months' supervision by the Probation Service and complete 120 hours' unpaid work.*
>
> ***Supervision period**: 12 months – D must be supervised by Probation and complete his unpaid work*
>
> ***Operational period**: 2 years – D must not commit any offences*
>
> *Sentence imposed if D breaks any of these terms: (up to) 9 months' custody.*

The court can periodically review D's progress.

Just as with a community sentence, if without reasonable excuse D has breached a requirement, the responsible officer **must give a warning** or initiate breach proceedings.

---

[132] ss.189-191 CJA 2003, as amended by s.68 LASPO 2012.

If D has already received a warning within the previous 12 months, the officer **must initiate breach proceedings**.

If D is brought to court for breaching the requirements of the supervision period or for being convicted of another offence during the operational period, the court has 3 options:[133]

- Activate the sentence in full (i.e. D must serve the full period of imprisonment to which he was originally sentenced);
- Activate the sentence in part (i.e. D must serve part of that sentence);
- Amend the order by adding or changing requirements or extending the supervision or operational periods.

There is a **presumption that the suspended sentence will take effect**, unless it will be unjust.

24.4 Mandatory and minimum sentences

Murger:
Where D is aged 21 or more and is convicted of murder, he will receive a mandatory sentence of **imprisonment for life**. The judge has **no discretion** in imposing this sentence. The judge will apply the usual sentencing principles to set a **tariff**, which is a minimum period of detention before D can be eligible for release. If D is released, he will spend the **rest of his life on licence**.

Trafficking Class A drugs:[134]
Where D is convicted of trafficking Class A drugs for the **third time**, he will receive a mandatory sentence of **at least 7 years' imprisonment**. The judge has **a discretion** to impose a lesser sentence where the circumstances would make this minimum sentence *"unjust"*.

Burglary:[135]
Where D is convicted of domestic burglary for the **third time** since 30 November 1999, he will receive a mandatory minimum sentence of **3 years' imprisonment**. The judge has **a discretion** to impose a lesser sentence where the circumstances would make this minimum sentence *"unjust"*.

---

[133] Sch.12 CJA 2003.
[134] s.110 PCC(S)A 2000.
[135] s.111 PCC(S)A 2000.

Firearms:[136]
　　　　　　　　　　　　Where D is convicted of a specified firearms offence he will receive a mandatory minimum of 5 years' custody if over 18, and 3 years if between 16-18. This is so **even where it is D's first conviction** of this type (or at all). The judge has **a discretion** to impose a lesser sentence in **exceptional circumstances** (not the same as *"unjust"*).

24.5 Principles applicable in determining the length of custodial sentences

A custodial sentence must be for the **shortest term that is commensurate with the seriousness of the offence**. The court can never impose a term higher than the permitted maximum for that offence.

Overall length will be determined by following the usual sentencing steps (see 22.9).

Any days D has spent remanded in custody will be deducted from his sentence automatically. Additionally, **half** the number of days that D has spent on a tagged curfew of **9 hours per day or more** (including the first but excluding the final day) whilst on bail normally will be deducted from D's sentence.[137] However, the judge must announce in court the amount of time spent on curfew that will count towards sentence.

24.6 Provisions as to early release and time spent on remand (outline only)

Prisoners serving sentences of 12 months or more (except for dangerous offenders, those sentenced to life imprisonment and those sentenced to an extended determinate sentence – see chapter 26) must be released on licence after serving half their sentence. This is subject to **standard** and **prescribed** conditions.

The standard conditions of licence include requirements that D:

- Keep in touch with the responsible officer;
- Permanently reside at an address;
- Not travel outside the UK without prior permission;
- Be of good behaviour;
- Not commit any offence;
- Undertake work only with the prior approval of the responsible officer.

Other conditions may also be imposed, e.g. a curfew or restrictions on D's freedom of movement.

---

[136] s.51A Firearms Act 1968.
[137] ss.240 - 240A CJA 2003.

If D breaches the conditions of his licence, it is likely to be revoked and D will be returned to prison.

25. Ancillary Orders and Costs on Conviction

Upon conviction, D can be ordered to pay a "just and reasonable" sum to cover P's costs. D's financial means will be taken into account.

The sum ordered should never be more than the costs actually incurred by P. If D pleads guilty, a costs order can still be made but it should be much less than a costs order made after a contested trial.

If a custodial sentence is passed on D, it is unlikely that he will receive a costs order as he will have no means to pay it.

If there are multiple Ds, the costs of trial can be split between them (see 8.7 and 9.10).

25.2 Compensation

The court **must** consider making a compensation order in any case where **personal injury, loss or damage has resulted from the offence**.[138] A compensation order can be made instead of or in addition to any other sentence.

Up to £5,000 compensation may be ordered in respect of each offence of which the offender has been convicted.

The court must make a compensation order wherever possible (subject to the V's views), and must give reasons if it decides not to order compensation. If D cannot afford to pay both compensation and a fine, **preference should be given to compensation**.

The court should consider two types of loss:
- Financial loss sustained as a result of the offence; and
- Pain, suffering or loss of amenity caused by any injury.

In determining the amount of compensation to be paid, the court should consider all factors that appear relevant (e.g. medical evidence and V's age and personal circumstances).

---

[138] s.130 PCC(S)A 2000.

25.3 Forfeiture and deprivation orders

The court can **deprive an offender of property** used to commit an offence or facilitate the commission of an offence. Before making the order, the court must have regard to the value of the property and the likely financial and other effects on the offender.

Where an offender is convicted of an offence under the Misuse of Drugs Act 1971, the court may order forfeiture and destruction of anything shown to the satisfaction of the court to relate to the offence.

25.4 Endorsement of driving licences and disqualification (outline only)

The court may disqualify any person convicted of an offence from driving for such period as it thinks fit.[139] This may be instead of or in addition to dealing with the offender in any other way, and the offence does not have to relate to driving (although disqualification is very rarely imposed for a non-driving offence).

Note that:

- Endorsement of a driving licence (i.e. awarding penalty points) is a mandatory punishment for most road traffic offences;
- Disqualification is a mandatory punishment for many more serious driving offences (e.g. dangerous driving and causing death by dangerous or careless driving).

If D receives 12 points on his licence, he must be disqualified under the "totting up" procedure.

There is a complicated body of statute and case law concerning **special reasons** (for mandatory disqualification) and **exceptional hardship** (for totting up disqualification), on which grounds D can avoid disqualification.

25.5 Registration of sex offenders

On conviction or caution for a specified sexual offence,[140] D will be subject to **notification requirements**.[141] This means that D's name will be entered into the Sex Offenders' Register and he must provide the police with the following information:

- Full name;
- Home address;
- Date of birth;

---

[139] s.146 PCC(S)A 2000.
[140] Any offence listed in sch.3 to the SOA 2003.
[141] ss.80-86 SOA 2003.

- National Insurance number;
- Vehicle details (if the offender has any vehicles): make, model, colour and registration number;
- Any information required by regulations made by the Secretary of State.

D must notify the police if any of the above information changes. D may also be required to inform the police when he intends to travel out of and return to the UK.

Where D has been convicted of a sexual offence overseas, the Magistrates' Court can, on application by police, make a **notification order**, imposing sex offender registration requirements on D.[142]

The amount of time D will be subject to notification requirements is as follows:

Sentence imposed / type of conviction	Notification period
<ul><li>Imprisonment for **30 months or more** (including imprisonment for life)</li><li>Imprisonment for public protection</li><li>Admission to hospital under a restriction order, or subject to an order for lifelong restriction</li></ul>	Indefinite
Imprisonment for **more than 6 months but less than 30 months**	10 years
Imprisonment for **6 months or less**, or admission to hospital without restriction order	7 years
Caution	2 years
Conditional discharge	The same as the period of discharge or probation
Any other sentence	5 years
Finite notification periods are halved if the person is under 18 when convicted or cautioned.	

---

[142] ss.97-103 SOA 2003.

25.6 Confiscation under the Proceeds of Crime Act 2002 (brief outline only)

*Where D has profited from his crime, the court may make a **confiscation order**. The aim is to deprive D of financial benefit obtained from criminal conduct. Such an order is a debt owed by D to the Crown and is enforceable in the courts. In brief, confiscation orders can be made where D has a general criminal lifestyle or has benefitted from general criminal conduct, or has benefitted from specific criminal conduct.*

The amount to be paid under a confiscation order must be paid on the date of the making of the confiscation order,[143] although the court may grant D up to 6 months to pay if necessary, and a further 6 months after that in exceptional circumstances.

If D fails to pay by the due date, interest will accrue,[144] at the rate specified in s.17 of the Judgments Act 1838.

---

[143] s.11 POCA 2002.
[144] s.12 POCA 2002.

26. The Dangerous Offender Provisions

26.1 How to identify specified offences

The *"specified offences"* to which the dangerous offender provisions may apply are:
- A violent offence specified in Part 1, **Schedule 15 of the CJA 2003**; or
- A sexual offence specified in Part 2, **Schedule 15 of the CJA 2003**.

A *"serious offence"* means a specified violent or sexual offence (i.e. that falls within the bullet points above), which is:
- Punishable with life imprisonment; or
- A determinate sentence of at least 10 years' imprisonment.

Serious offences are relevant NOT to the labelling of D as a dangerous offender, but to the imposition of certain types of sentence (see 26.3).

26.2 The principles involved in the assessment of dangerousness

For D to be considered a dangerous offender there must be:

> A **significant risk** of D
> committing further **specified offences** (whether serious or not)
>
> **and**
>
> A **significant risk** to members of the public
> of **serious harm** being caused by these offences

The risk in each case **must be significant**, and the potential harm caused **must be serious**. Serious harm means death or serious personal injury, whether physical or psychological.[145]

The court must obtain a PSR before deciding that the offender is dangerous; the court is guided but not bound by the findings of the PSR.

In so deciding, the court will look at many factors, e.g.:
- The background and circumstances of the current offence;
- D's socio-economic situation, accommodation, employment, any history of substance abuse, etc;

---

[145] s.224(3) CJA 2003.

- D's offending history;
- D's attitude towards his offending.

26.3 The nature of and conditions for the imposition of life sentences, imprisonment for public protection and extended sentences under the dangerous offender provisions

Note that imprisonment for public protection (IPP) has been **abolished** under LASPO 2012. Old-style extended sentences have also been abolished and replaced with the **extended determinate sentence** (EDS).

There are a number of sentencing options which a court can impose where D is assessed as a dangerous offender, which do not necessarily apply to ordinary Ds:
- A mandatory life sentence for serious offences;
- A mandatory life sentence under the *"two strikes rule"*; and
- An extended determinate sentence.

Life sentences

Under s.225 CJA 2003 the court **must** impose a life sentence where:
- D is a dangerous offender (see above); and
- D's crime was a **serious offence**; and
- D is over 18; and
- The maximum penalty for his offence is life imprisonment; and
- The offence is so serious that a life sentence is justified.

Under s.224A CJA 2003 (the *"two strikes rule"*),[146] the court must impose a life sentence where:
- D is convicted of an offence in Schedule 15B CJA 2003 (a list of serious sexual and violent offences); and
- The court would otherwise impose a custodial sentence of 10 years or more for the offence; and
- D had previously been convicted of a Schedule 15B offence; and
- For that previous offence, D was sentenced to a custodial sentence of at least 10 years, or a life sentence with a tariff of at least 5 years.

However, this rule does not apply when it would be **unjust** given any circumstances which relate to:
- The present offence; or
- The previous offence; or
- D.

---

[146] Inserted by s.122 LASPO 2012.

Extended sentences

An extended sentence (also called an *"extended determinate sentence"* or EDS) = D receives a custodial term and an **extension period**, which is a longer period **on licence** which starts running after the end of his custodial term (see 24.6).

Under s.226A CJA 2003, the court **may** impose an extended sentence where:
- D is convicted of a specified offence; and
- The court assesses D as a dangerous offender; and
- The court is not obliged to impose a life sentence under the *"two strikes rule"*; **and either:**
  - D had previously been convicted of a Schedule 15B offence; or
  - The current offence justifies a custodial term of at least 4 years.

Where D receives an EDS, he will be eligible for release after he has served **three-quarters of his term** (rather than half, as for ordinary prisoners). However, where D is sentenced to an EDS of ten years or more, or he is convicted of a Schedule 15B offence, then he will not be automatically eligible for release after three-quarters, but will be referred to the Parole Board who will decide if D is still a danger to the public.

IPP

IPP is a sentence of imprisonment for an indeterminate period, i.e. D does not know when he will be released.

*s.225 CJA 2003: the court **may** impose a sentence of IPP where:*
- *D is a dangerous offender (see above); and*
- *D's crime was a **serious offence**; and*
- *D is over 18; and*
- *A life sentence is not available or not justified; and*
- *Either:*
  - *D has a previous conviction for an offence from Schedule 15A CJA 2003; or*
  - *The current offence justifies a notional minimum term of 2 years' imprisonment (notional minimum = the amount of time D will actually serve. It is normally half the actual term imposed).*

Section 6

Appeals

27. Appeals from the Magistrates' Court

27.1 The power of the Magistrates to rectify mistakes

Under **s.142** of the Magistrates' Court Act 1980, the Magistrates may rectify certain mistakes they make in the course of proceedings. This is the equivalent of the *"slip rule"* in civil procedure. The Magistrates can:

- **Correct a mistake in sentence** (e.g. if they passed a sentence beyond their powers); or
- **Rehear the case** in front of a different bench.

s.142 only applies to criminal procedure, and not to any civil matter the Magistrates may deal with.

Applications under s.142 can be heard by the same or a different bench. However, s.142 cannot be used where:

- The Crown Court has already determined an appeal against the sentence, order or conviction which is disputed, or against any related sentence or order; or
- The sentence or order has already been dealt with by the High Court by way of case stated.

27.2 The general right of appeal from the Magistrates' Court to the Crown Court

Appeal from the Magistrates' Court lies to the Crown Court.[147]

Permission to appeal is not needed: there is an **automatic right of appeal**. Appeal can be against conviction or sentence.[148] An appeal against conviction is made where D believes that the Magistrates reached the wrong factual conclusions; an appeal against sentence is made where D believes that the Magistrates passed too harsh a sentence.

However, if D pleaded guilty, he cannot appeal against conviction, unless:

- The guilty plea was equivocal (see 4.2); or
- The guilty plea was made under duress.

D can of course appeal against sentence after a guilty plea.

---

[147] For procedure generally see CrimPR Part 63.
[148] s.108 MCA 1980.

27.3 The procedure in the Crown Court for dealing with the appeal, including the constitution of the Court

The appellant should send the notice of appeal **within 21 days** to both the Magistrates and the P. Time runs from the date of the decision which is being appealed.

The appellant should set out:
- The decision being appealed (i.e. the conviction or the sentence);
- A summary of the issues in the case;
- Which witnesses he wants to call;
- How long the trial lasted and how long the appeal is likely to last;
- Whether he has asked the Magistrates to reconsider the case;
- A list of those on whom he has served the notice of appeal.

The appeal is **heard by a judge together with 2 to 4 lay justices**. In a Youth Court, the lay justices must be authorised to sit in the Youth Court.

An appeal against conviction is simply a **rehearing of the proceedings in the Magistrates' Court**, i.e. it takes the form of a full trial. Both sides can call new evidence and witnesses if they wish. The Crown Court judge is not bound by any findings of fact made in the Magistrates' Court.

An appeal against sentence takes the form of a fresh sentencing hearing (i.e. a second chance to deliver a plea in mitigation).

27.4 The powers of the Crown Court on appeal, including the power to increase sentence

The Crown Court when hearing an appeal from the Magistrates' Court may:[149]
- Dismiss the appeal;
- (If against conviction) allow the appeal and quash the conviction (i.e. acquit D);
- (If against sentence) allow the appeal and vary the sentence. The correct procedure is to determine whether the sentence imposed was correct (i.e. not just within the discretion of the tribunal, but actually the right and just sentence for the case).

The **Crown Court can also increase the sentence** up to the maximum that the Magistrates could have passed.

---

[149] s.48 SCA 1981.

Where there has been **an error of law or jurisdiction, both sides** may appeal to the High Court by way of case stated.[150] This means to present the High Court with the facts of the case, the arguments made, and the question of law or jurisdiction on which the Magistrates have allegedly erred. The High Court will then answer the question posed.

Leave (= permission) is not required to appeal by way of case stated.

Note that an appeal by way of case stated does not reconsider the facts: an appeal against the factual conclusions reached by the Magistrates lies to the Crown Court (see 27.2 and 27.3).

There must have been a "final determination" in the case (i.e. conviction or acquittal). The hearing itself is in front of the Divisional Court (2 or more High Court judges). It comprises legal argument based on the stated case: **no live evidence is heard.**

Stating a case will extinguish the right of appeal to the Crown Court.

The Court can:
- Replace conviction with acquittal;
- Remit the case back to the Magistrates with a direction to convict and sentence D;
- Convict D itself;
- Remit the case back to the Magistrates with a direction to continue with the trial (where D was acquitted not after full trial, e.g. after a submission of no case to answer).

Where there has been **an error of law, an error of jurisdiction or a breach of natural justice, both sides** may appeal to the High Court by way of judicial review. The procedure is to bring a claim under Part 54 of the Civil Procedure Rules (i.e. a claim form setting out grounds, accompanied by written evidence). The D is the Magistrates' Court.

Permission for judicial review is required; it is considered by a single High Court judge.

In determining a judicial review, the Court can:[151]
- Make a quashing order (= quash the decision of the Magistrates' Court);
- Make a mandatory order (= require the Magistrates' Court to do something);

---

[150] s.111 MCA 1980.
[151] s.31 SCA 1981.

- *Make a prohibiting order (= prevent the Magistrates' Court from doing something);*
- *Substitute its own decision for that of the Magistrates' Court, but ONLY where there was an error of law, and without the error only one conclusion could be reached.*

28. Appeals from the Crown Court

28.1 The power of the Crown Court to rectify mistakes as to sentence

The Crown Court can rectify any mistake as to sentence or any other order **within 56 days** of the date on which the sentence was passed or the order made.[152] This allows mistakes to be corrected without the need to make an appeal to the Court of Appeal.

28.2 The right to appeal to the Court of Appeal

D can appeal against conviction or sentence. This is not an automatic right: **D requires leave to appeal** (see 28.3).

If D pleaded guilty, he cannot usually appeal against conviction, unless:
- The guilty plea was equivocal or mistaken; or
- As a result of an incorrect ruling on the law where the facts were admitted, D was left with no choice but to plead guilty.

An appeal can be brought even after D's death.

The principle of double jeopardy dictates that once acquitted, D should not face further prosecution for the same allegations. However, since 2003, **P can appeal against an acquittal in extremely exceptional circumstances**: [153]
- The offence was serious; and
- New evidence has come to light which is reliable, substantial, and highly probative; and
- A prosecution would be in the interests of justice; and
- P could not have found or used this new evidence before (e.g. scientific evidence which was not obtainable using the technology available at the time of the original acquittal).

28.3 The requirement to obtain leave to appeal to the Court of Appeal

Leave (= permission) to appeal to the Court of Appeal is required, unless the trial judge issues a certificate that the case is *"fit for appeal"*.[154] Such certificates are exceptional. An application for leave to appeal must be served on the Crown Court office **within 28 days** of the date of conviction, sentence or order being appealed; the Registrar then

---

[152] s.155 PCC(S)A 2000, as amended by s.47 and sch.8 paragraph 28 of the Criminal Justice and Immigration Act 2008.
[153] ss.75-97 CJA 2003.
[154] s.1(1) CAA 1968, as amended by s.1(1) CAA 1995.

passes it on to the Court of Appeal. There is no need to serve the application on P (who becomes the respondent).

28.4 The more common grounds that can give rise to appeal against conviction and sentence

Conviction

There is only one broad ground of appeal against conviction in criminal cases to the Court of Appeal: **that the conviction is unsafe**,[155] e.g. because there were:
- Errors in the course of the trial (e.g. wrongful admission of evidence);
- Errors in the summing up;
- Errors in the investigative or trial preparation process (e.g. disclosure failures);
- Other abnormalities (e.g. jury misbehaviour).

Not every error will result in the conviction being unsafe.

Sentence

An appeal to the Court of Appeal against sentence can take place either after trial on indictment, or following committal for sentence from the Magistrates' Court.

There are no statutory grounds for an appeal against sentence, but case law provides the following grounds:
- That the sentence is wrong in law (i.e. *ultra vires*);
- That the sentence is wrong in principle (i.e. the wrong form of sentence, e.g. custodial when the threshold is not passed);
- That the sentence is *"manifestly excessive"* (greater than any reasonable judge would have given);
- That the judge took the wrong approach to sentencing (i.e. the judge ignored relevant mitigating factors or considered irrelevant aggravating factors);
- That there has been a procedural error.

---

[155] s.2 CAA 1968.

28.5 The procedural requirements for applying for leave under the Criminal Procedure Rules, including the practical steps that counsel should take when advising and preparing grounds of appeal

The application for leave to appeal must be **lodged at the Crown Court within 28 days of conviction or sentence**, whichever is being appealed.[156]

The Registrar then passes the application to the Court of Appeal. An application for leave to appeal should set out in a single document:
- What is being appealed;
- Each ground of appeal, and a summary of each supporting argument;
- The facts of the case;
- Any relevant authorities;
- For appeal against conviction: any transcript which the court will need in determining the appeal (e.g. a transcript of the judge's summing up);
- For appeal against sentence: the court's sentencing powers.

It is counsel's responsibility to put forward only reasonably arguable grounds.

The application for leave to appeal is then considered **by a single judge of the Court of Appeal, on the papers** (i.e. without a hearing).

Alternatively, counsel can apply for **a certificate that the case is fit for appeal** from the Crown Court judge, immediately after the conviction or sentence which is being appealed. Counsel must:
- Make an **immediate oral application** to appeal after conviction or sentence; and
- Apply **in writing within 14 days**, in the same manner as the appeal notice outlined above.

Bail

It is rare for D to be granted bail pending appeal when he would otherwise be in custody, as it is considered undesirable to release someone after a conviction.

However, it will be granted in exceptional circumstances, such as where:[157]
- The appeal is likely to be successful; or
- The sentence will have been served by time appeal is heard.

If leave to appeal was granted by the Crown Court by way of a certificate, the Crown Court has jurisdiction to grant bail. If (as is more common), leave is sought from the Court of Appeal, the appellant will have to apply to the Court of Appeal for bail. The bail

---

[156] For appeals to the Court of Appeal generally, see CrimPR Part 68.
[157] *R v Watton* (1979) 68 Cr App R 293.

application will also be considered by the single judge at the same time as he considers the application for leave.

28.6 Renewal of application before full court after a refusal by single judge

If the single judge refuses to grant leave to appeal, that decision can be challenged by renewing the application to a sitting of the Court of Appeal.[158]

D must notify the court of an intention to renew the application **within 14 days**, although this can be extended.

28.7 The power of the Court to make a loss of time direction

The Court of Appeal can direct that time D spends in custody pending the determination of his appeal will not count towards his custodial sentence.[159] This is known as a **loss of time direction**.

Loss of time directions are used when D renews an application for leave to appeal which is **wholly without merit**, after it has been rejected by the single judge. They are a disincentive to hopeless appellants, intended to stop the court becoming blocked up with unmeritorious appeals.

The Court of Appeal may not make a loss of time direction where:
- Leave has already been granted; or
- The trial judge issued a certificate that the case was fit for appeal; or
- The case was referred by the Criminal Cases Review Commission.

28.8 The rules concerning the Court of Appeal hearing fresh evidence during the appeal

An appeal to the Court of Appeal generally takes the form of submissions on the law; it is rare for the Court of Appeal to hear evidence at the appeal. Evidence will be heard on appeal where it is **necessary or expedient in the interests of justice** to do so.[160]

In so deciding, the Court of Appeal will consider whether:
- The evidence appears capable of belief;
- It may afford any ground for allowing the appeal;
- It would have been admissible at trial;

---

[158] s.31 CAA 1968.
[159] s.29 CAA 1968.
[160] See s.23 CAA 1968 for the Court of Appeal's general powers to hear evidence on appeal.

- It is an issue which is the subject of the appeal;
- There is a reasonable explanation for the failure to adduce it.

Evidence is generally only heard on appeal when it is fresh evidence, i.e. evidence not presented in the original proceedings, usually because it did not exist or was not available then.

28.9 The principles and procedure the Court of Appeal will adopt when determining appeals against conviction and sentence

An appeal against conviction will be heard by **at least 3 judges**. The court can:
- Dismiss the appeal;
- Quash the conviction (= acquit D);
- Quash the conviction but order a retrial,[161] if the interests of justice so require;
- Substitute a conviction for an alternative offence[162] as long as the jury **could** and **would** have found D guilty of this (i.e. only when the jury **must have been satisfied of the facts which make D guilty of the other offence**, and when the alternative charge would have been available to them).

An appeal against sentence will be heard by **at least 2 judges**. The court can:
- Dismiss the appeal;
- Quash the sentence and pass a new sentence.[163] The court **cannot impose a harsher sentence,** and its sentencing powers are limited to those of the Crown Court.

If D was convicted of 2 or more offences, the court can raise one sentence as long as the total is not greater than the original sentence.

In any appeal, the Court of Appeal can hear any evidence it wishes to hear.[164]

28.10 Consequences of a conviction being quashed, including ordering retrials

When a conviction is quashed, it is effectively rendered void. The Court of Appeal has the power to order a retrial after quashing a conviction, where the interests of justice require. This is usually where D's conviction must be quashed (e.g. because of a procedural irregularity), but where there is strong evidence of his guilt.

---

[161] s.7 CAA 1968.
[162] s.3 CAA 1968.
[163] s.11 CAA 1968.
[164] s.23 CAA 1968.

28.11 Attorney General's references on points of law and references of unduly lenient sentences

An Attorney-General's reference is a form of appeal **made by P**. There are two types:

- A reference **on a point of law**: made after D has been acquitted. It is not to challenge the acquittal, but **to clarify the law**. The Attorney-General (or more often counsel acting on his behalf) will formulate a question of law for the Court of Appeal to determine. The Court of Appeal's judgment on the law has no bearing on the acquittal of D, but shapes the law for future cases.

- A reference of an **unduly lenient sentence**: made after D has been sentenced. It is made where the Attorney-General considers the sentenced passed to be so lenient as to *"fall outside the range of sentences which judge, applying all relevant factors, could reasonably consider appropriate"*. Only sentences passed in the Crown Court can be the subject of a reference, and only for indictable-only or either-way matters. If the reference is successful, the Court of Appeal will substitute the appropriate (increased) sentence.

The Attorney-General needs **leave from a single Court of Appeal judge** to bring a reference. Application for leave to appeal must be made **within 28** days of conviction or sentence, whichever is relevant.

28.12 Prosecution appeals against trial judge rulings

P cannot appeal against an acquittal (except in the very limited circumstances outlined at 28.2). However, CJA 2003 gave P the right to appeal against the following rulings made by the trial judge:

- Terminating rulings (= any ruling that has the effect of bringing the proceedings to an end);[165]
- *Evidentiary rulings (= any ruling relating to the admissibility or exclusion of P evidence in prescribed circumstances – not in force as at 31 December 2013).*[166]

28.13 The Criminal Cases Review Commission (brief outline only)

The Criminal Cases Review Commission is a public body which investigates possible miscarriages of justice. It examines convictions and sentences and decides whether to refer them to the Court of Appeal.

---

[165] s.58 CJA 2003.
[166] s.62 CJA 2003.

28.14 Appeals to the Supreme Court (outline only)

The Supreme Court is the highest appellate court. It hears appeals from the Court of Appeal on points of **general public importance**.

Permission to appeal is required; applications for permission to appeal will be considered on the papers by a panel of at least 3 judges.

CPSIA information can be obtained at www.ICGtesting.com
Printed in the USA
LVOW12s1649250214

375113LV00002B/343/P

9 781291 227314